Presented To:

Michelle

From:

Darryl Hall

Date:

3-21-15

Bless you

Exploring

your *Dreams*

and

Visions

DESTINY IMAGE BOOKS BY JAMES W. GOLL

The Seer
The Lost Art of Pure Worship
PrayerStorm
Dream Language
Exploring the Nature and Gift of Dreams

Exploring
your *Dreams*
and
Visions

*Receive and Understand
your Dreams, Visions, and
Supernatural Experiences*

Personal Revelatory Journal

James W. Goll

DESTINY IMAGE® PUBLISHERS, INC.
P.O. Box 310, Shippensburg, PA 17257-0310
"Promoting Inspired Lives."

This book and all other Destiny Image, Revival Press, MercyPlace, Fresh Bread, Destiny Image Fiction, and Treasure House books are available at Christian bookstores and distributors worldwide.

For a U.S. bookstore nearest you, call 1-800-722-6774.
For more information on foreign distributors, call 717-532-3040.
Reach us on the Internet: www.destinyimage.com.

ISBN 13 TP: 978-0-7684-0315-2

For Worldwide Distribution, Printed in the U.S.A.
1 2 3 4 5 6 7 8 / 16 15 14 13 12

Dedication

With gratefulness, we dedicate this study guide to Jesus—our Dream Come True!

Endorsements

One of the reasons I love *Exploring Your Dreams and Visions* is because not only does it teach you about dreams, but this book actually helps you in the process of remembering your dreams. We are entering a season where the Lord is restoring the power of the night watch in the Church. We will be arising and praying as well as sleeping and receiving! I believe James has created a tool that will be used from one generation to another generation as each wield the sword of revelation to build the Church for the future and unlock the Kingdom of God. *Exploring Your Dreams and Visions* is an excellent source of experiential and practical principles that will assist you in learning to rule the night.

Chuck D. Pierce
President, Glory of Zion International, Inc.
Vice President, Global Harvest Ministries

James Goll has blessed us with vital truths and living examples to understand and fulfill dreams. The reader will discover the real purpose and meaning of dreams. Biblical and practical guidelines are given to help an individual discern whether the dream was divinely given and how to properly apply its meaning. *The Dream Language Journal* will be another wonderful tool. James, thanks for helping us to understand and fulfill our spiritual dreams.

DR. BILL HAMON
Apostle, Bishop of Christian International Ministries Network

Francis Bacon said, "Reading maketh a full man; speaking, a ready man; writing, an exact man." After reading James' *Dream Language* and the new journal I would add, "and dreaming, a complete man." Those dreams I once dismissed now have meaning, and I have the prophetic guide, James Goll, to thank. For God speaks in the language of image, symbol, color, and sense, and nobody does a better job of explaining the prophetic realm and its language than James Goll.

DR. LANCE WALNAU
Lance Learning Group

Everyone is dreaming! It's just one of the languages of Heaven. If we are to interpret the signs and the times, then we need master technicians to help us. It has been my great pleasure to know and work with James Goll over the years. I cannot think of anyone more spiritually prepared or experienced in the pragmatics of dream language than this man. I have heard him teach on intrinsic and extrinsic dreams in particular—brilliant! That alone is worth the price of this book and now the accompanying journal. If you're a dreamer, then interpreting dream language is a must. This is the material that will put wings under the feet of the process that you need to move quickly into that new land of the Spirit that awaits.

GRAHAM COOKE

James Goll is a superb writer and he has delivered marvelously on a very pertinent topic for these days. The Bible has much to say about dreams, and James helps put the whole topic into clear perspective for us. His *Dream Language Journal* will be an additional great tool.

PAT WILLIAMS
Senior Vice President, Orlando Magic

Contents

Foreword

THE ETHEREAL VAPORS OF OUR dreams will become tangible existence when we write them out and believe anything is possible with God. God is the giver of dreams. God is also a redeemer. So, like a knight in shining armor, He comes to restore the dreams we have allowed to fall by the wayside. He inspires us to recall the images He sent long ago. God has mapped out our future. He brings the events of the world to bear on our individual circumstances as He wills. When the events of our life coincide with the correct timing of His plans, the next phase of our destiny ensues. God knows the perfect time to bring the dreams and plans He has formulated to enable our purpose to come to pass.

Dr. James Goll knows the voice of the Holy Spirit as few men do. He has built a vast repertory from his expertise in the spirit realm. His knowledge of the areas of the prophetic, dream interpretation, and intimacy with God in prayer propelled him to develop *The Dream Language Journal* as a wonderful tool to enable us to record our dreams and visions in a constructive, detailed way.

Dreams are God's love letter to us. They allow us to see the plans and purposes God had for us before we entered into this earthly realm of existence. All of our days were numbered and ordered by God before we were born. Part of our spiritual journey is learning how to record or journal our days so that we enter into the divine scripts of success that have already been written for each of us. As we scribe our dreams in detail and journal as the Holy Spirit reveals their hidden interpretation, the once obscure visions gain clarity so our life is enriched. When we record and treasure the dreams God sends, He will continue to reveal His goodness and mercy to us in the night season. *The Dream Language Journal* will become one of your most prized possessions. As you journal daily, it will be filled with God's eternal wisdom and His personal answers to your heartfelt questions.

DR. BARBIE L. BREATHITT
Author of *Dream Encounters, Gateway to the Seer Realm,* and *Dream Seer*

Lesson One

Journaling as a Tool of Retaining Revelation

DO YOU NEED HELP RETAINING what you have already received? Then I have a simple remedy for you—journal! Yes, it is one of those awesome spiritual disciplines! Journaling is a tried and tested spiritual tool that will help you retain revelation and grow in your capacity to discern the voice of the Holy Spirit. I have tried it, and it works!

Basically, journaling is simply a method of keeping notes for future reference. It can take many forms. Your journal may consist of your prayers, a record of God's answers as you perceive them, and/or a record of what you sense the Holy Spirit is saying to you through His various delivery systems. Journaling is a fundamental and clearly useful biblical discipline.

Some believers express concern that journaling is an attempt to put subjective revelation on the same level of authority as Scripture. This is not the case at all. The Bible *alone* is the infallible Word of God. Journaling is just another tool to help us retain and be more faithful with what He speaks to us.

God speaks to His children much of the time! However, we do not always differentiate His voice from our own thoughts, and thus we are timid at times about stepping out in faith. If we clearly learn to retain what He is speaking to us, we will know that He has already confirmed His voice and Word to us. Thus we will be enabled to walk out God's words to us with greater confidence. Journaling then becomes a way of sorting out God's thoughts from our own.

As it has been for so many, the simple art of recording revelation may prove to be one of the missing links in your own walk of hearing God's voice. Continuity of language, divine suggestions and reminders, and also learning the proper interpretation of symbols will occur as you use journaling as a creative tool of storing up and later deciphering revelation.

I strongly encourage you to start journaling now if you have not already done so. The principles, tips, and suggestions in this chapter will help you get off to a strong start. Those of you who are already engaged in journaling, I urge you to continue!

To encourage you as to the value of journaling, let me share some thoughts on the subject from another elder friend, Herman Riffel. Herman is one of the "patriarchs" of modern-day visionary revelation—an authority not only on dreams and their interpretation but also on journaling as an effective method of retaining revelation.

> In life we keep the treasures we value. Unwanted mail that comes is tossed away with just a glance. But bills, whether we like them or not, are carefully laid aside until we pay them. Checks are deposited in the bank so that no money is lost. Diplomas and certificates of recognition are hung on the wall for others to see.
>
> What do we do with the promises the Lord gives us? They are worth more than any amount of money. What happens to the lessons we have learned through difficult and costly

experiences? Too often we forget within a day or two the words of encouragement God gave us. The promises vanish away in the midst of new problems, unless we make a proper record of them.

I know by personal experience. Lillie and I pray for our children regularly, often for specific needs. Then we wait on the Lord for His answer, and graciously He gives us a word of encouragement.

Recently one of these words came to us: *Salvation shall spring forth like the grass and you will rejoice with joy unspeakable, for I will do what I have promised. Therefore, wait in patience and trust in Me, for I am faithful.*

This was an encouraging word and we did rejoice in it. Just a few days later, however, I asked Lillie if she remembered what the promise was that God had given. She did not remember, and neither did I, for problems had absorbed our attention again. Since I keep a journal, however, we were able to check it, find the promise, and again receive encouragement.[1]

A Personal Note

One of the treasures I found upon the departure of my dear late wife, Michal Ann, was her personal, revelatory journals, sitting in her night stand beside our bed. To my delight, I found the original handwritten notes telling of her nine weeks of angelic visitations in the early 1990s. In it she wrote how the Holy Spirit promised her that next time He came to visit her, not only would the angels come, but Jesus Himself would come for her. It brought such comfort to me to realize this is exactly what had happened. Jesus Himself had come for her. Her journals gave me comfort, insight, and hope.

Therefore, I urge you to begin keeping a journal if you are not already doing so. What to include in a personal spiritual revelatory journal? One of the first things we may record in the day are our dreams from the night before. Some use digital recorders and others use computers; devices today help in their journaling experience. I still use notebooks and "journals" for the most part. I write down the date, the place I am in, the time I woke up and the summary of the experience. Often later, I reflect on it, after prayer and waiting on the Lord, and compose a short potential application of the prophetic experience.

We may record a Scripture which God speaks to us that day. A burden, a heartfelt urgency as well as dreams and visions and visitations may be noted. You see, your journal is a track record of your spiritual adventure, not simply a diary to record daily activities. So we take time to listen to what God is saying to our hearts. We might meditate on the Scriptures, or we might sit in contemplation before our Lord Jesus Himself. We learn to "waste time on Jesus," from the world's viewpoint, in order to hear what God wants to say to us.

I'm glad my Annie left me a journal! Now I have a treasure chest full of jewels that I can go back to and glean the many lessons He was teaching us those many years ago. The Lost Art of Journaling is a key to receiving and retaining revelation. Ready to start! Let's get going!

Note

1. Herman H. Riffel, *Learning to Hear God's Voice* (Old Tappan, NJ: Chosen Books, 1986), 147-148.

Lesson Two

Discipline or Privilege?

S UCH IS THE PRINCIPLE OF journaling. Obviously, there are
many different forms of journaling. Our focus in this book is on
journaling our dream and vision language, but we can journal many
other aspects of our Christian lives. There are prayer journals and
daily devotional journals, for example. People keep different types of
journals for different purposes.

Some people would describe journaling as a spiritual discipline. I
prefer another term. Like many others, I have used the phrase "spiritual discipline" for years to describe any habitual practice we undertake
to facilitate spiritual growth. When composing my book *The Lost Art
of Practicing His Presence*, however, the Holy Spirit said to me, "You're
not disciplined enough to have a spiritual discipline." That nailed me!

"Okay," I replied, surprised and a little miffed. (Deep in my heart,
though, I knew He was right.)

He said, "These are spiritual privileges." That put a whole new
angle on things. I really like the phrase, "spiritual privileges," because
that is what they are. Looking at them as privileges rather than as disciplines completely changes your mindset because doing something

as a discipline can sometimes lead to a performance-based mentality. Doing the same thing as a privilege, however, means doing it because you can do it, because you see the value in doing it, because God enables you to do it, and because you want to do it—not because you have to do it to please God or stay on His "good side." It becomes a matter of perspective, like the difference between saying the glass is half empty or half full. Praying, studying, fasting, worshiping—they are all amazing spiritual privileges—with great benefits!

Lessons From Habakkuk and Daniel

Journaling our spiritual experiences has clear biblical precedent. Several times in the Book of Revelation, John is instructed to record what he sees. In fact, the entire Book of Revelation itself is a divinely inspired record of a series of awesome and incredible visions that John saw while "in the Spirit on the Lord's day" (Rev. 1:10).

The discipline of spiritual journaling appears also in the Old Testament. Consider, for example, these words from the prophet Habakkuk:

> I will stand on my guard post and station myself on the rampart; and I will keep watch to see what He will speak to me, and how I may reply when I am reproved. Then the Lord answered me and said, "Record the vision and inscribe it on tablets, that the one who reads it may run. For the vision is yet for the appointed time; it hastens toward the goal and it will not fail. Though it tarries, wait for it; for it will certainly come, it will not delay" (Habakkuk 2:1-3).

Habakkuk is seeking a spiritual experience. He is seeking to hear the *Rhema* voice of God directly in his heart so that he can understand what he sees around him. First of all, he goes to a quiet place where he can be alone and become still. Second, he quiets himself within by "watching to see" what God would say. Last of all, when God begins to speak, the first thing He says is, "Record the vision." Habakkuk wrote down what he was sensing in his heart. The benefits of this type of journaling were retained for years to come so that those who would later read it would be able to "run with it." Often the vision is fulfilled by others, so here we have another great benefit: If the revelation is preserved, then another group, city, or even generation can learn the lessons and move forward themselves.

Daniel was another biblical prophet who journaled. In fact, the seventh chapter of the Book of Daniel is essentially Daniel's journal entry regarding a significant and powerful dream:

> *In the first year of Belshazzar king of Babylon Daniel saw a dream and visions in his mind as he lay on his bed; then he wrote the dream down and related the following summary of it* (Daniel 7:1).

If you read Daniel's account of his dream in the rest of the chapter, you'll find that Daniel did not write down all the details of his amazing and rather intense dream. While in a spirit of rest, he composed a summary of his encounter. Too many people get caught up in the microscopic details in their sincere attempts at journaling and thus end up missing the primary emphasis of their visitation. Be like Daniel—write down a summary and keep it simple! The Holy Spirit will have a way of bringing back to your remembrance the details you might need later.

I take enormous encouragement from the life of Daniel. His style of journaling particularly appeals to me. Daniel's life spanned almost the entire 70-year period of the Babylonian exile. The events recorded in the Book of Daniel cover much of that same period of time, yet it is only 12 chapters long. Obviously, Daniel did not record everything he experienced; or, at least, not everything he recorded has survived to come down to us today. The Book of Daniel records the highlights, the most spiritually significant events in the life of Daniel and his people. A lifetime of experience is condensed into 12 short chapters—a summary, as it were.

When it comes to journaling, here's the bottom line: Do what works for you. I can give you plenty of practical tips, but in the end you have to decide what you feel most comfortable with. Perhaps you like to write and are good at it; you may prefer to record a full account of your dreams and experiences. However, if you lack the time or inclination to write long accounts, do what Daniel and other prophets did and write a summary. Set down the simplest, most basic sequence of events as a framework for recording in detail the highlights in the most salient or significant points. Whatever—make it simple, practical, and attainable. Amen and Amen!

Lesson Three

Properly Interpreting Revelation

SOME YEARS AGO I WAS traveling through the night by train from the Frankfurt, Germany region to Rossenheim in southern Bavaria. I was in one of the sleeping cars but, unable to sleep, I spent much of my time praying in the Spirit. The Holy Spirit kept speaking to me over and over, "Where are My Daniels? Where are My Esthers? Where are My Josephs, and where are My Deborahs?"

After many years of pondering on this word, I believe that the Holy Spirit is on a quest to find believers He can work with—believers who will dream God's dreams at any cost, have a discerning spirit to properly interpret the times, and who learn to intercede out of a posture of revelation.

Daniel, Esther, Joseph, and Deborah were godly people who possessed the spirit of revelation and who altered destinies and changed history through the revelation that was bestowed on them. They trusted the Lord for wisdom and insight and served His purposes in their generation. Today the Spirit of God is looking for like-minded and like-hearted individuals who will be the Daniels, the Esthers, the Josephs, and the Deborahs for their day.

Like the biblical heroes before them, these modern-day trailblazers will study to show themselves approved as workmen for God, rightly dividing the word of truth (revelation) that is given to them (see 2 Tim. 2:15 KJV). And, like their Old Testament counterparts, they will learn to speak the language of that revelation in a manner that is relevant to their contemporaries.

What Language Do You Speak?

Before you can interpret your dreams and visions properly or intercede effectively from the posture of revelation, you must understand the language of that revelation. In his book on dreams, Mark Rutland issues this caution:

> Believers must, of course, be cautious when seeking to understand dreams and even more prudent when acting on them. There is no substitute for wisdom and discernment in dream interpretation, and prayer is crucial to developing both. Believers should commit their subconscious minds to the Lord as well as their waking thoughts, then seek from God, in earnest prayer, understanding for the visions of the night.[1]

What language do you speak? Have you learned your spiritual alphabet? Your spiritual alphabet will be unique to you. God will speak revelation to you according to the language you speak. Doctors, nurses, and other medical and health professionals have a language all their own, a technical vocabulary that untrained laypeople cannot understand. Music has a written language that is incomprehensible to anyone who has never been taught to read the symbols. Pastors have their own language, too. This can cause problems when their language does not match that of their congregations!

What language do you speak? Whatever your language is, the Holy Spirit will speak to you in that language. Of course, I am not talking so much about languages like English, French, German, Russian, or Spanish, as I am the "language" with which we interpret life. Because each of us has different life experiences, the language by which we receive and impart revelation will be distinct to each of us. We each have a personal walk and, in a sense, a personal talk. Our spiritual alphabet, though similar, is unique to each individual.

Regardless of how our individual spiritual alphabets differ, our basic approach to interpretation should be the same. Proper interpretation can occur on many different levels. Here are three simple steps for interpreting your dream revelation:

1. Study the interpretation of words and symbols by researching their meanings as recorded in Scripture and other historical literature. Find out how biblical characters and other figures from the past interpreted these words and symbols in a dream context. This is an excellent (and probably the easiest) way to begin.

2. Develop the habit of journaling. Effective interpretation is a skill that is learned over time and with experience. Your spiritual alphabet is unique to you. Journaling will help you capture your distinct pictures, grant understanding over time, and give wisdom for your journey.

3. Welcome the anointing, gifting, and presence of the Holy Spirit. He will guide you into truth, keeping things safe yet adventurous and pure yet unreligious.

In your eagerness to reach step three, don't bypass steps one and two. Always begin with the Scriptures. Let the Bible be its own best commentary. God will never contradict His Word. Let His written Word give you insight into the meaning of His visionary revelation. Study it thoroughly. Pray over it. Lay a solid foundation of the Word in your life to give the Holy Spirit something to breathe upon.

Interpreting dreams is like putting together a giant jigsaw puzzle with thousands of tiny pieces that must be fitted together in exactly the right order. The quickest way to complete a jigsaw puzzle is to start with the border—the framework—and the same is true with dream interpretation. Once you have the framework in place it becomes easier to see where the rest of the pieces go. Before long, the big picture begins to take shape. At least, that's the way it usually works for me. I ask the Holy Spirit to give me a thought or a word. He sheds His light on one thing, which leads me to another, and another, and then everything just starts to click.

Interpretations Belong to God

The cardinal rule to keep in mind when properly interpreting dreams and visions is that "interpretations belong to God." He who gives you the spirit of revelation is also the one who gives you the capacity to interpret that revelation. Here are some biblical examples:

From the life of Joseph:

> Then they said to him, "We have had a dream and there is no one to interpret it." Then Joseph said to them, "Do not interpretations belong to God? Tell it to me, please" (Genesis 40:8).

Imagine being in the place where you are so sure that interpretations belong to God and so absolutely confident in His anointing that, like Joseph, you could say to someone, "Tell it [your dream] to me," and know that God would give you the interpretation!

From the life of Daniel:

> As for these four youths, God gave them knowledge and intelligence in every branch of literature and wisdom; Daniel even understood all kinds of visions and dreams. ...As for every matter of wisdom and understanding about which the king

consulted them, he found them ten times better than all the magicians and conjurers who were in all his realm (Daniel 1:17,20).

Daniel was even given the ability to interpret the handwriting on the wall that King Belshazzar saw, which foretold the king's death under God's judgment (see Dan. 5:1-31).

Although it may not come out in Aramaic or Hebrew or Greek or English or Spanish, God writes in signs to His people and He wants to give us the capacity to interpret the signs of the times. We need to pray for the Lord to release in our own day godly people of wisdom who can interpret the handwriting on the wall for our generation.

From the life of Issachar:

Of the sons of Issachar, men who understood the times, with knowledge of what Israel should do, their chiefs were two hundred; and all their kinsmen were at their command (1 Chronicles 12:32).

Two hundred chiefs "who understood the times" held an entire tribe under their command. How? People will follow a person who has revelation. People will be drawn to anyone who walks with integrity in the spirit of wisdom and revelation.

The more you learn how to listen and recognize the voice of the Spirit of God, the more He will enable you to operate on multiple levels of insight. God is the master multitasker and He can enable you to be a multitasker as well. You can listen on more than one level. You can listen to the heart of a person, you can listen to the realm of the soul, and you can listen to the Holy Spirit. It requires a fair measure of grace and the ability to block out the noise of friction, static, and distractions, but all things are possible.

What God did before, He wants to do again! Right here, right now!

Note

1. Mark Rutland, *Dream* (Lake Mary, FL: Charisma House, 2003), 59.

Lesson Four

Revelation Is Full of Symbolism

D REAMS AND VISIONS ARE OFTEN the language full of emotions
and therefore contain much symbolism. We must learn to take
our interpretations first from Scripture and then from our own lives.
Throughout Scripture God is consistent with His symbolic language.
The symbolism He uses in Genesis will be similar to that found in
Revelation. In fact, one of the fundamental principles of biblical interpretation is the "law of first use." This simply means that how a word
or image or symbol or type is used in its first appearance in Scripture
is a key to how it should be interpreted throughout the Bible. This
consistency in symbolic language runs true in our own lives as well.

Let me explain a little further. In the Bible, the number six often
is used as a symbol for mankind. How do we know this? Refer back
to the first chapter of Genesis. What happened on the sixth day of
creation? Man was created. Day six is the day of man. Now let's go
to the other end of the Bible, to the Book of Revelation. There we
find the reference to the number 666, which is plainly identified as
"the number of a *man*" (Rev. 13:18 NKJV). In the Greek there is no
definite article preceding the word for "man" in this verse, so it could
also be translated simply as "the number of man." The number 666

represents a false trinity, the exaltation of man—humanism being worshiped as a god. In both Genesis and Revelation, therefore, the number six is associated with mankind.

Here is another similar example. What happened on the seventh day of creation? God rested because He had finished His creative work. Therefore, the number seven is the number of rest or completion. According to the four Gospels combined, how many statements did Jesus make from the cross? Seven. The last of these was, "It is finished!" (John 19:30). Jesus had finished His work; He had completed His mission. Now He could rest. Throughout the Bible the number seven is symbolically associated with rest and completion.

A similar principle applies when God speaks revelation to you. When He first introduces a word or a symbol or an image to you in a dream, you may not understand it in the beginning. But you will get it eventually, and that word, symbol, or image will become part of a pattern. Once it is introduced into your spiritual alphabet, it will become consistent in its meaning for you.

For example, let's say that you have a dream in which an apple appears and you discern through the Holy Spirit that it symbolizes Israel because Zechariah 2:8 refers to Israel as the "apple" of God's eye. Once the image of the apple has entered your spiritual alphabet as a symbol for Israel, you can be confident that whenever that image appears in a future dream, the dream has something to do with the nation of Israel. God is consistent with His revelatory symbolism.

Three Realms for Interpretation of Symbols

When seeking interpretation of symbolic dream and vision language, the first place you should look *always* is in Scripture. The Bible is full of parables and allegories from which to draw types, shadows, and symbols. Here are some examples: the mustard seed as a metaphor for faith (see Matt. 13:31-32); incense representing the prayers of the saints (see Rev. 5:8; 8:3-4); seed as a symbol for the Word of God (see Luke 8:11); and candlesticks symbolizing the church (see Rev. 1:20). If your dream has the same symbolic image as one found in the Bible, chances are it has the same meaning.

After Scripture, a second place to look for interpretation of your revelatory symbols is in colloquial expressions that fill our memory bank. The Holy Spirit turns these into pictorial language. God takes these "sayings" and idioms and uses them to speak spiritual truth. One example of this is found in Judges 7:9-15 where a barley cake appears to Gideon in a dream. Since Gideon had spent much of his life as a thresher of wheat and barley, the barley cake was a symbol from his colloquial spiritual alphabet and had distinct meaning to him.

In the same way, God will speak to you with colloquial expressions that are familiar to you but might not be to someone else. If you are from the northern or northeastern part of the country, your colloquialisms will be different than those of someone from the Deep South, and God will speak to each of you accordingly.

The third realm for interpreting these prophetic symbols comes from our own personal revelatory alphabet. This is similar to the second realm in that the objects or symbols do not mean the same thing to you as they would to someone else. Even in the Bible the same symbol or image sometimes means something different depending on how it is used or who receives it. These exceptions, however, do *not* violate the law of first use.

God often works more than one way at a time. And sometimes the symbol or image involved has more than one facet or aspect, which allows for some variations in meaning. Context determines interpretation.

The Bible uses the image of a lamb in several different ways. In Isaiah, the Messiah is presented as a *Lamb* led to the slaughter. John's Gospel presents Jesus as the Good Shepherd and His disciples as *little lambs.* The Book of Revelation reveals Jesus Christ the *Lamb* as a Conqueror. Spiritually speaking, all three of these images are true to a lamb's nature: it is led to the slaughter, it follows its shepherd, and it conquers in the end by walking in humility because the meek will inherit the earth.

Actual Versus Visual

Insights, revelations, warnings, and prophecies from the Lord may come in supernatural *visual* dreams or in *actual* dreams.[1] *Visual* dreams are visual revelations that do not involve as much active participation on the part of the dreamer as with an actual visitation from the Lord. The dreamer simply observes and receives the message. These visual dreams may contain more symbols, mysteries, and obscurities than do other types of revelation.

Actual dreams are those in which God's tangible presence is evident in some way. To see the Lord in a dream is *visual*, but for the Lord to *manifest* Himself to you in a dream is *actual*. If you dream something angelic and sense that same presence when you wake up, it was more than just a *visual symbolic* dream. The angels were *actually* there. Quite often this will reveal itself in the form of a riveting awareness all over your body of a divine presence in the room. But if there was *no* such manifested presence when you awakened, then the dream was simply *visual*, although it may still contain a wonderful message from God.

A manifestation of blessing, healing, deliverance, or endowment of power requires an *actual* visitation from the Lord in some form. Such manifestations involve an impartation of God's anointing, which will manifest in the natural realm. Therefore, an *actual impartation* occurs and the person actively participates although his or her body is asleep.

I have vivid memories of some dream encounters that I call "the Bread of His Presence" dreams. In one of them I was carrying loaves of bread and was searching for the little mint-green blanket that belonged to our daughter Rachel. Rachel loved that blanket and for quite a few years carried it with her just about everywhere she went. In my dream, I found Rachel's blanket and wrapped the loaves of bread in it. I held them closely to my chest and noticed that the bottom of each loaf was a little satin napkin that looked like a diaper.

This was an *actual* dream because there was an *actual* presence in the room. I was asleep, but the Holy Spirit was very active. Even asleep I was talking out loud and prophesying. This was more than just a message I passively received. I declared, "Just as we parents learn to love, nurture, care for, and cherish our newborn child, so should we as believers care for, love, and cherish the bread of God's presence; then revival will come."

When I woke up, my arms were outstretched over my chest as though I was clutching those loaves of bread tightly to my chest as if they were my very own babies, wrapped in my daughter's blanket. Even as I woke I heard myself prophesying, "When we as parents will care for, love, and nourish the bread of His presence, like a parent does his newborn child, then we will have revival." In fact, I was the one who was being revived. I loved God's presence just as I had our newborn child. Though I did not see any angels in the room upon waking, the manifested presence of God was so strong you could almost cut it with a knife! Yes, let's love the bread of His presence!

Some of our experiences are full of symbolism and others…well, they are just flat out another dimension. God shows up and shows off. When that happens, how do you write that down? With as much emotive passion as possible! God Himself still comes to visit His kids! Let it be so!

Note

1. For more information on this subject, see James Goll, *The Seer: The Prophetic Power of Visions, Dreams, and Open Heavens* (Shippensburg, PA: Destiny Image Publishers, Inc., 2004).

Lesson Five

Some Basics of Revelatory Interpretation

Now it is time to get down to some "nuts and bolts" basics of revelatory interpretation. The first principle to keep in mind is to *reduce the revelatory experience to its simplest form*. With too much detail you could miss the interpretation. That is like not seeing the forest for the trees. Keep it simple. Otherwise, you risk obscuring the meaning. Take the dream to its simplest form and build on that.

Next, remember that *context determines interpretation*. The meaning is not always the same every time. For example, a seed can mean faith, the Word, the Kingdom of God, a future harvest, etc. There are no steadfast formulas. The things of the Spirit are "spiritually discerned," not naturally discerned (1 Cor. 2:14 NKJV).

Third, *determine whether a series of repetitious dreams is involved.* Did you have two, three, or four dreams, or are they all different aspects of the same issue? More than one dream in the same night is often just a different look or version of the same message. Joseph in the Book of Genesis had two dreams, each with different symbols, but both dreams had the same meaning. Whether it was sheaves of wheat in the field or the sun, moon, and stars in the heavens, both dreams meant that the members of Joseph's family would one day bow down to him. Joseph's dreams related to his destiny.

If you don't understand that repetitive dreams typically relate to the same subject matter, you will end up looking at them as entirely isolated dreams that have no connection to each other. In doing so you risk misinterpreting all of them. If you experience repetitive dreams, look for a common thread of meaning.

Analyze your dream by asking a series of basic questions. First, *are you observing?* Where are you in the dream? If you are in the observation mode, then the dream probably is not primarily about you. It is about someone or somewhere else. God does nothing without a witness observing issues. If you are an observer in your dream, then you are that witness. This might even mean that you are going to be a watchman or an intercessor in the situation.

Second, *are you participating?* Are you actively participating in the dream but still not the main figure? Then the dream still is not primarily about you, even though its meaning may touch you more directly than when you are merely an observer.

Third, *are you the focus?* Is everyone watching you? If you are the focus of the dream, then one of the first things you need to do is try to identify where you are. That will help you frame out the dream so all the pieces can be put into place.

Fourth, *what are the objects, thoughts, and emotions in the dream?* Are there words in the dream? What impressions and thoughts are you left with when you remember or are awakened by the dream? What is the intensity of the dream—the main emotion? You will know intuitively what the most important issues are.

Interpreting Colors

Understanding the significance and use of colors is one of the key principles to proper interpretation. Colors can have both a good and positive meaning as well as an opposite bad or negative meaning. Remember, context is the key! Dreams are full of these understandings; they are often descriptive parables of light. Let's go to *The Seer* book for some illustrations. Here are some representative examples:

1. *Amber*—the glory of God (Ezek. 1:4; 8:2 KJV).

2. *Black*—sin, death, and famine (Lam. 4:8; Rev. 6:5; Jer. 8:21).

3. *Blue*—Heaven, Holy Spirit (Num. 15:38).

4. *Crimson/Scarlet*—blood atonement, sacrifice (Isa. 1:18; Lev. 14:52; Josh. 2:18,21).

5. *Purple*—kingship, royalty (John 19:2; Judg. 8:26).

6. *Red*—bloodshed, war (Rev. 6:4; 12:3; 2 Kings 3:22).

7. *White*—purity, light, righteousness (Rev. 6:2; 7:9).

Interpreting Numbers

Like colors, numbers are highly significant both in the Bible as well as in dreams. So it is important to learn a few basic principles for interpreting numbers. If you internalize and follow the principles, they will help preserve you from interpretation error or extremes.

1. The simple numbers of 1-13 often have specific spiritual significance.

2. Multiples of these numbers, or doubling or tripling, carries basically the same meaning, only they intensify the truth.

3. The first use of the number in Scripture generally conveys its spiritual meaning (the law of first use).

4. Consistency of interpretation—God is consistent, and what a number means in Genesis is the same thing that it means through all Scripture to Revelation.

5. The spiritual significance is not always stated, but may be veiled, or hidden, or seen by comparison with other Scriptures.

6. Generally, there are good and evil, true and counterfeit, godly and satanic aspects in numbers.

Getting a little more specific, let's look at the numbers 1-13 and their possible symbolic meanings:

1. One: God, beginning, source (Gen. 1:1).

2. Two: witness, testimony (John 8:17; Matt. 18:16; Deut. 17:6).

3. Three: Godhead, divine completeness (Ezek. 14:14-18; Dan. 3:23-24).

4. Four: earth, creation, winds, seasons (Gen. 2:10; 1 Cor. 15:39).

5. Five: Cross, grace, atonement (Gen. 1:20-23; Lev. 1:5; Eph. 4:11).

6. Six: man, beast, satan (Gen. 1:26-31; 1 Sam. 17:4-7; Num. 35:15).

7. Seven: perfection, completeness (Heb. 6:1-2; Judg. 14; Josh. 6).

8. Eight: new beginning (Gen. 17; 1 Pet. 3:20; 2 Pet. 3:8).

9. Nine: finality, fullness (Matt. 27:45; Gen. 7:1-2; Gal. 5:22-23; 1 Cor. 12:1-12).

10. Ten: law, government (Exod. 34:28).

11. Eleven: disorganization, lawlessness, antichrist (Dan. 7:24; Gen. 32:22).

12. Twelve: defying government, apostolic fullness (Exod. 28:21; Matt. 10:2-5; Lev. 24:5-6).

13. Thirteen: rebellion, backsliding, apostasy (Gen. 14:4; 1 Kings 11:6).

Two Other Factors to Consider

Our revelatory experience and thus its interpretation is also affected by our culture. There are cultural and social interpretations that we must bring into our understanding as well: West versus East; North versus South; North American versus South American; European versus African; Middle Eastern versus Asian; Chinese versus Russian, etc. The degree to which you have to consider these cultural factors will depend on your sphere of influence. The larger your sphere, the more significance these cultural elements will have for you.

Another critical key to dream interpretation that is sometimes overlooked is the discipline of meditating on the Word of God:

> *When I remember You on my bed, I meditate on You in the night watches* (Psalm 63:6).

> *I will meditate on all Your work and muse on Your deeds* (Psalm 77:12).

> *I will meditate on Your precepts and regard Your ways* (Psalm 119:15).

> *I remember the days of old; I meditate on all Your doings; I muse on the work of Your hands* (Psalm 143:5).

Take the time to gain understanding of the principles and metaphors of Scripture. Like the psalmist, meditate on them day and night. They can have many layers of meaning. They do with me, and by learning the ways of the Spirit, I am sure they will for you!

Lesson Six

Keeping Interpretation Simple

Walking in a prophetic language and this amazing revelatory culture is a form of tapping into the mind and heart of God and can be an exciting and exhilarating journey. But understanding and interpreting the revelation He gives in dreams and other spiritual encounters can often be a complex and even confusing process. Therefore, let me summarize what we have discussed in a handful of concise statements that will make everything easier to remember.

1. Most of all, dreams should be interpreted on a personal basis first (John 10:3).

2. Most dreams should not be taken literally. They need interpretation (Dan. 1:17; Gen. 40:8).

3. God will use familiar terms that you know (Matt. 4:19).

4. Ponder on the dream or revelation and ask the Holy Spirit for insight (Dan. 7:8; 8:15-16; Luke 2:19; 1 Cor. 2:12-14).

5. Ask the Holy Spirit what the central thought, word, or issue is in the revelation. Reduce the dream to its simplest form. What is the main thought?

6. Search it out in the Word. Dreams from the Lord will never go against His written Word (Prov. 25:2).

7. What did you sense and feel from the dream? Was it a good or evil presence? What was the primary emotion?

8. Relate the dream to your circumstances and spheres of influence.

9. Consecutive dreams often have similar meanings (Gen. 41:1-7, 25-31). God will speak the same message more than once in more than one way.

10. What are the colors? Is everything black and white with one main object in color?

11. Interpretations can be on three levels: personal, church, or national and international.

12. More than one interpretation can come forth in one dream. Just as with Scripture, there is the historical context as well as the personal, present implication. So it is with dreams. It might be a general word for the church with specific applications for yourself (or others).

13. Some dreams may only be understood in the future. They unfold over time. Details will make sense down the road.

14. Write down in a journal the summary; date it; write down where you were, the time (if you woke up from it), the main emotions, and a possible interpretation.

15. The key to proper interpretation is to ask questions, questions, questions!

Finally, remember that dreams are significant to all! "There couldn't be a society of people who didn't dream. They'd be dead in two weeks."[1] To receive a dream is the human obligation that begins to move a divine purpose from the mind of God to become reality in human history.[2]

Dreams and visions are where space and time are pushed away, where God allows our inner selves to see beyond and behind the conscious plane and where possibilities and hopes, as well as all our hidden monsters, come out, come out wherever they are.

> "Dreaming permits each and every one of us to be quietly and safely insane every night of our lives."[3]

But life is more than dreams. As author Mark Rutland says:

> If we idolize the primary mental image and cling to it too tenaciously, we may well despise the realization of the dream when it finally arrives. An overly cherished fantasy has the capacity to steal our joy and even blind us to the dreams for which we have longed.[4]

In closing, let us consider the cautionary wisdom of "The Preacher" in Ecclesiastes:

> *For in many dreams and in many words there is emptiness. Rather, fear God (Ecclesiastes 5:7).*

Father, we know that dreams and visions and their interpretations belong to You. With honor coupled with a deep hunger, we ask You to give us Your wisdom applications, in Jesus' great name, amen.

Notes

1. "William S. Burroughs Quotes," Goodreads.com, accessed April 07, 2012, http://www.goodreads.com/quotes/show/55251.

2. Rutland, *Dream*, 8.

3. "William C. Dement Quotes," Goodreads.com, accessed April 07, 2012, http://www.goodreads.com/quotes/show/49000.

4. Rutland, *Dream*, 38.

Lesson Seven

The Twenty Most Common Dreams

VARIOUS MINISTRIES AND ORGANIZATIONS HAVE logged literally thousands of dreams and therefore have been able to decipher the most common dreams that people have. The following is a partial listing of these most common types of dreams. This list is not comprehensive, and the dreams are not listed in any particular order. In other words, they are not ranked by most common to least common or by any other ranking factor.

I. Dreams of Your House

This one would easily rank in the top five most common dreams. Virtually all of us have had one or more dreams in which our house appears, either the house we currently live in or one where we once lived in the past. The house normally represents your life, and the circumstances taking place in the house reflect the specific activities in your life. These dreams may also represent a church as well.

Individual rooms of the house may represent specific things. For instance, if the bedroom appears, the dream may have something to do with issues of intimacy. The bathroom may represent a need for cleansing. The family room may be a clue that God wants to work on family relationships, either your nuclear family or your church family. This is one of the most common dreams that my wife has had over the years.

2. Dreams of Going to School

These dreams often center on the taking of tests. The tests may be for the purpose of promotion. Or you might find yourself searching for your next class—an indication that guidance is needed or a graduation has just occurred. You might be repeating a class you took before, possibly meaning that you have an opportunity to learn from past failures. High school dreams may be a sign that you are enrolled in the School of the Holy Spirit (H.S.=High School=Holy Spirit). There are limitless possibilities. These are just a few examples. Interesting enough, the Teacher is always silent when giving a test!

3. Dreams of Various Vehicles

These may indicate the calling you have on your life, the vehicle of purpose that will carry you from one point to another. Cars, planes, buses, etc., may be symbols of the type or even the size of the ministry you are or will be engaged in. That's why there are different kinds of vehicles. Note the color of the vehicle. If it is a car, what is the make and model? Observe who is driving it. Are you driving or is someone else driving? If someone else is driving, who is it? Do you know the person? Is it a person from your past? If the driver is faceless, this may refer to a person who will appear sometime in your future or that the Holy Spirit Himself is your driving guide.

4. Dreams Concerning Storms

Storm dreams tend to be intercessory, spiritual warfare-type dreams. They are particularly common for people who have a calling or gift in the area of the discerning of spirits. These dreams often hint of things that are on the horizon—both dark, negative storms of demonic attack for the purpose of prayer, intercession, and spiritual warfare, as well as showers of blessing that are imminent.

5. Dreams of Flying or Soaring

Flying dreams deal with your spiritual capacity to rise above problems and difficulties and to soar into the heavenlies. These are some of the most inspirational and encouraging in tone of all dreams. When awakening from a dream where you fly or soar, you often wake up feeling exhilarated—even inebriated—in the Spirit. Ascending-type dreams are more unusual yet edifying. Remember, we are seated with Christ Jesus in the heavenly places far above all principalities and powers.

6. Dreams of Being Naked or Exposed

These dreams indicate that you will be or are becoming transparent and vulnerable. Depending on your particular situation, this may be exhilarating or fearful and could reveal feelings of shame. Note: these dreams are not meant to produce embarrassment but rather draw you into greater intimacy with the Lord and indicate places where greater transparency is required. These types of dreams often appear during times of transition where you are being dismantled in order to be re-mantled.

7. Dreams of the Condition of Your Teeth

Often, these dreams reveal the need for wisdom. Are your teeth loose, rotten, falling out, or are they bright and shiny? Do you have a good bite? Are you able to chew your cud? Teeth represent wisdom, and often teeth appear loose in a dream. What does that mean? It may mean that you need a wisdom application for something you are about to bite off. The fear of the Lord is the beginning of wisdom.

8. Dreams of Past Relationships

This kind of dream may indicate that you are being tempted to fall back into old patterns and ways of thinking. Depending upon who the person is in the dream, and what this person represents to you, these dreams might also be an indication of your need to renew your former desires and godly passions for good things in life.

Seeing a person from your past does not usually mean that you will literally renew your old relationship with that individual. Look more for what that person represents in your life—for good or bad. A person who was bad in your life may represent God's warning to you not to relapse into old habits and mindsets that were not profitable. On the other hand, a person who was good in your life may represent God's desire or intention to restore good times that you thought were gone.

9. Dreams of Dying

These dreams are not normally about the person seen in the dream in a literal sense, but are symbolic about something that is passing away or departing from your life. The type of death may be important to note. Watch, though, to see if resurrection is on the other side.

Not long ago I had a dream where I was observing my own funeral. Because I was battling cancer at the time, this dream really shook me up for a while until the Lord showed me what it really meant. I was back in my hometown in Missouri, driving a white pickup truck. My mom and dad, who are both in Heaven, were in the truck with me. I drove by our old Methodist church and saw a white hearse outside. I watched as pallbearers dressed in black brought a white casket out of the church and placed it into the hearse. Upon awakening, I realized that I was watching my own funeral.

The dream was in black and white rather than color, which was a clue to its true meaning. God was tipping me off to the enemy's desire to place a spirit of death in my thoughts. The Lord was actually strengthening me to stand against this disease as well as the spirit of death behind it. Wage war with the dreams of insight that the Lord gives to you. Fight the enemy's plans in Jesus' name! By the way, I did wage war and won the battle!

10. Dreams of Birth

Normally these dreams are not about an actual childbirth but rather about new seasons of purpose and destiny coming forth into your life. If a name is given to the child, pay close attention because that usually indicates that a new season in the purposes of God is being birthed. While I say this, there are exceptions. I remember so fondly, when my wife was pregnant with our third child, Tyler Hamilton, that she had a dream that she gave birth to a little girl named Rachel. I told her that was a symbolic dream. But true to form, she was right and I was wrong—child number four came along, and her name, of course, is Rachel!

11. Dreams of Taking a Shower

These are cleansing-type dreams (toilets, showers, bathtubs, etc.) revealing things that are in the process of being flushed out of your life, cleansed and flushed away. These are good dreams, by the way. Enjoy the showers of God's love and mercy and get cleansed from the dirt of the world and its ways. Apply the blood of Jesus and get ready for a new day!

12. Dreams of Falling

These dreams may reveal a fear you have of losing control of some area of your life or, on the positive side, that you are actually becoming free of directing your own life. What substance you fall into in the dream is a major key to proper understanding. The outstanding primary emotions in these dreams will indicate which way to interpret them. Falling can be fearful, but it can also represent falling into the ocean of God's love.

13. Dreams of Chasing and Being Chased

Chasing dreams often reveal enemies that are at work, coming against your life and purpose. On the opposite side, they may indicate the passionate pursuit of God in your life, and you toward Him.

Are you being chased? By whom? What emotions do you feel? Are you afraid of getting caught? Or maybe you are the one doing the chasing. Who are you chasing? Why? Again, what emotions do you feel during the chase? The answers to these questions and, particularly, the dominant emotions in the dream will often help determine the direction of its interpretation. Often the Lord appears in various forms, motioning to us, saying, "Catch Me if you can!"

14. Dreams of Relatives, Alive and Dead

Most likely, these dreams indicate generational issues at work in your life—both blessings and curses. You will need discernment as to whether to accept the blessing or cut off the darkness. This is particularly true if grandparents appear in your dreams, as they will typically indicate generational issues.

One night I had a dream in which I saw my grandfather standing on the porch of his old country house, dressed in his overalls. His white hair was shining, and he had an incredible smile on his face. To this day I am still pondering over the full meaning of this dream. My grandfather may have been a symbol for God the Father, the Ancient of Days, appearing on the front porch of our family house drawing us unto Himself.

15. Dreams Called Nightmares

Nightmares tend to be more frequent with children and new believers in Christ, just as calling dreams do. They may reveal generational enemies at work that need to be cut off. Stand against the enemies of fear. Call forth the opposite presence of the amazing love of God, which casts out fear, for fear has torment!

16. Dreams of Snakes

The snake dream is probably one of the most common of all the categories of animal dreams. These dreams reveal the serpent—the devil with his demonic hosts—at work through accusation, lying, attacks, etc. Other common dreams of this nature include dreams of spiders, bears, and even alligators. Spiders and bears are the two other major animals that appear in dreams that show fear. The spider in particular, releasing its deadly poison, is often a symbol of witchcraft and the occult.

17. Dreams of Dogs and Cats

After snakes, the most common animal to appear in dreams is the dog. A dog in your dream usually indicates friendship, loyalty, protection, and good feelings. On the other hand, dog dreams may also reveal the dark side, including growling, attacking, biting, etc. Sometimes these dreams reveal a friend who is about to betray you.

Dreams with cats are also quite common. These dreams also vary in nature with everything from the feeling of being loved, to being smothered, to persnickety attitudes, the occult, and even witchcraft.

18. Dreams of Going Through Doors

These dreams generally reveal change that is coming. New ways, new opportunities, and new advancements are on the way. Similar to dreams of doors are dreams including elevators or escalators, which indicate that you are rising higher into your purpose and your calling.

19. Dreams of Clocks and Watches

Clocks or watches in a dream reveal what time it is in your life, or the need for a wake-up call in the Body of Christ or in a nation. It is time to be alert and watchful. These dreams may indicate a Scripture verse as well, giving a deeper message. Are you a watchman on the walls? If so, what watch are you on?

20. Dreams With Scripture Verses

Sometimes you may have a dream in which Bible passages appear, indicating a message from God. This phenomenon may occur in a number of ways: verbal quotes where you actually hear a voice quoting the passage, digital clock-type readouts, and dramatizations of a scene from the Bible, just to name a few. Quite often these are watchmen-type dreams, dreams of instructions filled with the ways of wisdom.

My dear Michal Ann had many encounters of this type. Her Bible was open and filled with all kinds of notes. Somewhere, somehow, she picked up on the number 111 but did not understand what it meant. When she woke up all she knew was that it somehow referred to Scripture. She searched her Bible for a little while but could not find the right passage. After asking the Holy Spirit for guidance, she fell asleep again and had a second dream. In this second dream, Mike Bickle, leader of the International House of Prayer in Kansas City, came up to her with his Bible open and said, "It is Colossians 1:11." Upon waking the second time, Michal Ann looked up the Scripture:

> [We pray] that you may be invigorated and strengthened with all power, according to the might of His glory, [to exercise] every kind of endurance and patience (perseverance and forbearance) with joy (Colossians 1:11 AMP).

That verse became a life message for Michal Ann. Why? She needed that word in her own life, and the Lord used her to give that word away, imparting it to release that nature of God in others. You can do the same! Learn your revelatory language and shift yours and other people's spiritual climates in Jesus' name!

Lesson Eight

People Who Appear

ANOTHER EXTREMELY COMMON OCCURRENCE IN dreams is the appearance of people—family members, friends, acquaintances, prominent leaders in church, society, or government and even complete strangers. In the majority of these cases, the people who appear in your dreams and/or visions are often symbolic in nature. Seeing a person in an encounter does not necessarily mean that you will have an encounter with that person.

There are three basic questions you can ask to help you interpret dreams in which certain people appear:

1. Who is this person in relation to you?

2. What does this person's name mean?

3. What character trait or calling does this person represent to you?

Although no list of people who appear in our dreams could ever be comprehensive, the list that follows cites the most common people or type of people whom you are likely to encounter in your dreams, along with their probable symbolism.

1. A man or woman of God in your life most probably represents a particular type of message being delivered. The important issue here is not who the person is but the message he or she bears. Focus in on the message. That is where you will most likely find the meaning behind the dream.

2. An untrustworthy person in your past may indicate a coming situation that you should not trust. Seeing someone in a dream from your past who is associated with a betrayal or a bad situation may be a warning from the Holy Spirit. These may be calls to prayer to cut off a bad situation.

3. A healing evangelist (prophetic person, etc.) appearing in your dream usually represents a healing grace that is coming your way. The identity of that healing evangelist or prophetic person is not as important as what he or she represents—the kind of ministry associated with that person.

4. A husband in your dream often means that Christ Jesus the Lord is drawing ever so close in a covenant relationship.

5. Getting married in a dream usually relates to growing intimacy with God or a new joining that is coming your way. Keep in mind, opposites attract.

6. Dreams with dead people in them speak of the common sentiment attached to those deceased loved ones. This is *not* an indication that you are "crossing over" or actually visiting this person from your past in order to receive guidance! Do not equate this with the error of seeking guidance from the spirits of the dead, as King Saul did with the spirit of Samuel (see 1 Sam. 28:1-25). God is simply giving you a snapshot of something that the dead person represents.

7. Dreams of presidents and other people in authority are often calls to pray for national events. I used to have dreams of President Clinton where he and I were walking

together and I would take his hand and suddenly be able to feel the condition of his heart. And then I would pray for him, interceding not only for his heart's condition but also for the burdens or challenges of our nation.

8.   A faceless person often appears in dreams as an indication of the presence of the Holy Spirit, or possibly even angels, in your life. Sometimes people dream of a faceless man driving a bus but they don't know who he is. This, too, often represents the Holy Spirit driving the bus of your life and steering you into your life mission.

R-rated Dreams—Am I Sick or What?

One aspect of dreaming that many people are embarrassed to talk about, much less admit to, is the aspect of dreams that contain sexual content and/or nudity. This is an important point as many people worry that if they have such occasional dreams it automatically means they have a dirty mind, a moral problem, or some such thing. Often, however, dreams with sexual content have nothing to do literally with sexual intercourse.

The difficulty with dealing with "R-rated" dreams is illustrated by the fact that several different schools of thought exist regarding these dreams and how they should be interpreted. Generally, there are four of these. Depending on one's point of view, sexually charged dreams are:

1.   A spiritual call to greater intimacy.

2.   A warning of one's need of cleansing of attitudes of the mind, motives of the heart, and/or even acts of immorality.

3.   A calling or a joining of union with another person or even people group.

4. Natural body dreams containing the biological and physical desires that are common to most people.

In actuality, sexual dreams cannot be confined to just any one of these four categories alone. All of them are valid at one time or another depending on the specific dream. When dealing with this kind of dream, allow for the possibility of it authentically being a body dream. It is not necessary always to spiritualize everything. Sometimes there is no spiritual content. Sometimes a dream is just a dream.

To aid you in understanding and interpreting dreams with sexual content, here are some important questions to consider:

1. Is it the same sex? Is it the opposite sex? Don't take the images at face value, particularly if same-gender sex is involved. Look for a higher meaning. For example, much of the church world breeds only after its own kind; we tend to only relate to those who are most like us. The dream may indicate a need to cross-pollinate with other members of the Body of Christ. Spiritual "inbreeding" leads to weakness and eventual extinction. Multiplication comes from sowing your seed into those who are opposite of you.

2. Is it an old love or a new love? This could indicate what you currently are passionate about. Are you being tempted to go back to something old? Is there something new on the horizon that you are becoming passionate about?

3. Does this person seem to take the place of the Lord? If so, there is a serious need for cleansing and dealing with issues of idolatry.

4. Does the dream leave you feeling dirty or clean? A dirty feeling probably means that cleansing and/or repentance of some kind are needed. Feeling clean usually points to a more positive interpretation.

5. Are you or others naked in the dream? Transparency is a good thing. But often in these dreams everyone can see what is going on in your life. These dreams are not to embarrass you but to encourage you in your vulnerability with others.

Additional Thoughts on the Subject

Dr. Joe Ibojie provides a slightly different slant in his book, *Dreams and Visions*:

> Sex in a dream suggests that you are probably making, or about to make, decisions based on a carnal nature. In Scripture, God frequently uses sexual immorality as an allegory for unfaithfulness, or deviation from spiritual truth. Frequent experience of sex in dreams speaks of carnality, but it also indicates a hidden, unbroken stronghold of lust. Rape indicates violation of the dreamer's person or integrity, and this must be averted in prayer.[1]

To further clarify the different ways that sexual dreams can be interpreted, here are some final thoughts from Joy Parrott:

> God is not a prude and He may give you some dreams that will have you sure they couldn't be from Him, yet they are. Of course, many of these will not be divine, especially if we continue to walk in the things of this world and satisfy our fleshly desires. Yet God has recorded some risqué things in the scripture which confirms that He is not a prude. In the book of Ezekiel, God refers to Jerusalem, His people, as harlots! In Hosea, God tells the prophet Hosea to marry a prostitute as a prophetic drama of His unconditional love for His people. God told Isaiah to run around naked for three years prophesying to everything in sight! ...Such examples show that God isn't concerned about

offending us or sparing our "holy ears" from hearing such things. God wants to speak to us and sometimes He will get downright blunt! He is going to speak in a language that we will understand.[2]

Understanding our dreams is one thing; interpreting them is another. In closing, however, let me leave you with a biblical promise and a thought related to understanding our dreams:

Call to Me and I will answer you, and I will tell you great and mighty things, which you do not know (Jeremiah 33:3).

Dreams do not explain the future—the future will explain the dreams. Ouch! That one stung just a bit! But just keep going on the journey with me. We will learn together as we keep on going on the road less traveled.

Notes

1. Dr. Joe Ibojie, *Dreams and Visions: How to Receive, Interpret, and Apply Your Dreams* (San Giovanni Teatino (Ch), Italy: Destiny Image Europe, 2005), 160.

2. Joy Parrott, *Parables in the Night Seasons: Understanding Your Dreams* (Renton, WA: Glory Publications, Joy Parrott Ministries, 2002), 58-59.

Lesson Nine

Tips on Remembering Revelation

SOME PEOPLE TELL ME THAT they do not hear from God in their lives—period! Others say they simply can't remember their revelatory experiences. Still others seem to remember only a fragment or portions of scattered images, which at the time do not seem to make much sense to them. But you were born to be a dreamer.

Sleep specialists tell us that everyone dreams for a period of time while in rapid eye movement (REM) sleep. So, in reality, all of us dream at some point every night. The issue then becomes one of knowing some practical tips and learning to rest under the anointing of the Holy Spirit in order to recall what we have been shown.

The Scriptures speak of the fleeting nature of dreams:

> *He flies away like a dream, and they cannot find him; even like a vision of the night he is chased away* (Job 20:8).

Daniel 2:1-47 expresses the frustration that Nebuchadnezzar, the king of Babylon, experienced as he received a detailed dream but could not recall it! The dream disturbed the king so much that he searched for relief and health! God heard his plea and sent Daniel who, after a season of seeking the face of God, related to the king not only his dream itself but also its interpretation. In reality, of course, it was God who revealed these things to Daniel. Daniel sought God's face, and God gave him the spirit of understanding. If you seek God's face the way Daniel did, God will do the same for you.

Of course, no commitment to journaling will do any good if you cannot remember your dreams. You will remember that we discussed this problem and some possible solutions in detail in chapters three and four. At this point, however, I would like to add a few practical tips for retaining revelation. These steps will enhance your ability to journal effectively and enable you to remember your dreams longer.

1. If possible, get rid of your loud alarm clock. Ask the Holy Spirit to help you wake up. Try to establish the habit of getting up at a set time. This requires discipline and will naturally be harder for some than for others.

2. Many dreams come between four and five o'clock in the morning. Whenever you awaken, learn to linger for a few minutes in a place of rest, if possible.

3. Instead of an alarm, consider waking to a clock radio tuned to soothing music. This is what I did for years. I got rid of the blaring alarm and woke up to classical music, which doesn't chase away dreams. Classical music actually helps create a soothing atmosphere conducive to dream retention. Worship music has the same effect, particularly the softer, more soaking, reflective styles.

Be prepared to record your revelations by observing a few practical tips:

1. Keep a note pad and a pen by the bed so you won't have to get up before you record your dream. A simple spiral notebook works fine.

2. This is a personal journal. Grammar, neatness, and spelling are not critical issues. Content is crucial!

3. Consider using a small tape recorder. Keep it by your bedside so that all you have to do is turn over and whisper into it.

4. Later in the day or week, consider word-processing the scribbles you previously captured. Some people transfer their experiences to a more permanent "journal." I keep both a personal dream journal and a ministry dream journal in my bag at all times!

5. Develop your dream alphabet by keeping track of symbols. Ask, "What does this symbol mean to me?" and "Can I find it in Scripture?"

6. Make note of your feelings/emotions in the dream/revelation. When you summarize your dream, be sure to describe how you felt during the dream, even if you include only a few words.

7. Be still and try to recall one or two of the details, and then your memory will kick in (see Zech. 4:1-2). Find one thread of the dream and then, in prayer, gently pull and more will appear on your screen.

8. Date all entries. This is important for many reasons, not the least of which is keeping track of patterns or progressions that may occur in your dream journey.

9. If traveling, record your location at the time of your dream. This can be just as important as the date. The locale may prove to be highly significant to interpreting your dream.

10. Expect God's love to be affirmed toward you. And then, as you receive it, expect the gifts of the Holy Spirit to be in operation.

Whenever possible, seek training and wise counsel from gifted interpreters of dreams. Not everyone will have this capacity as well developed as others. Even in Scripture, Daniel and Joseph are the only ones who are specifically mentioned as having this gift. Just as in the New Testament we have the gift of speaking in tongues, but corresponding to it we have the gift of interpretation of tongues. Ask for the interpretation! You have not because you ask not! Just ask!

Lesson Ten

Practical Applications of Quietness

A<small>RE YOU READY FOR ONE</small> of the most hidden and significant keys to unlocking the world of revelation in your life?

One primary principle in retaining revelation is to learn to be still before the Lord—to quiet our mind and spirit and wait on Him. It says in Psalms, *"Be still, and know that I am God"* (Ps. 46:10 KJV). Years ago, the Holy Spirit taught me that stillness is the incubation bed of revelation. Quietness can actually be a form of faith because it is the opposite of anxiety and worry. Many times that is easier said than done. So, just how do you learn to become still before God?

I'll try to answer. First, remove external distractions. Mark 1:35 says that Jesus went to a secluded place to pray. Find a place where you can get away. For me, when I was growing up, I would get away by taking long walks. My family lived in a rural community in northwest Missouri. There were railroad tracks less than 300 yards from our house, and I used to get on those tracks and walk for miles. Hour after hour I would walk and talk to God. Outdoors and alone was the best place for me to have my communal time with the lover of my soul. Distractions were minimal. I could talk to God and listen to Him talk to me.

I have to fight for this alone time today. But whether it is a walk in the hills of Franklin, Tennessee, lingering in my bed with the covers pulled over my head, sitting in my special chair, or quieting my soul while listening to my favorite soaking CD, nothing takes the place of time alone with God!

Second, you must quiet your inner being. One of the biggest challenges in this will be your mind's tendency to suddenly remember all sorts of things that you need to do. The best way to counter that is by taking a few moments to write down all those things so that you can remember to do them later. Then, put them out of your head. Your mind should be at rest on those matters because you have taken action and not simply tried to ignore them. Release your personal tensions and anxieties to the Lord, *"casting all your anxiety on Him, because He cares for you"* (1 Pet. 5:7). Finally, focus your meditating on the person of Jesus. Yes, focus on Jesus!

In becoming still, you are not trying to do anything. You simply want to be in touch with your Divine Lover, Jesus. Center on this moment of time and experience Him in it. All of these things will help you silence the inner noise of voices, thoughts, pressures, etc., that otherwise would force their way to the top. This grace of becoming still before God is often referred to as contemplative prayer.

Quietness has a great deal to do with your having a spirit of revelation in your life. Commit yourself to creating a spiritual culture where the Holy Dove will want to come and stay. Pull down the shades over the windows of your soul. Enter the Holy of Holies in your heart where Jesus the Messiah lives. Yes, He has taken up residence within you! He is there, and He is waiting to commune with you.

You are now a candidate to receive revelation! In some way, *Rhema* is couched in vision. The Book of Habakkuk opens with the words, *"The oracle* [or burden] *which Habakkuk the prophet saw"* (Hab. 1:1). The prophet quieted himself to *watch* and see what the Lord would speak. As we have seen, focusing the eyes of our heart upon God causes us to become inwardly still. It raises our level of faith and expectancy and results in our being more fully open to receive from God.

Wisdom Ways With Journaling

Any venture into new territory is fraught with perils and pitfalls; receiving and retaining revelation is no different. Here are some practical safeguards to help protect you as you embark on your adventure.

1. Cultivate a humble, teachable spirit. Never allow the attitude, "God told me, and that's all there is to it." All revelation is to be tested. You will make mistakes. Accept that as a part of the learning process and go on.

2. Have a good working knowledge of the Bible. Remember, *Rhema* is based on *Logos*. The revelatory never conflicts with the written Word!

3. God primarily gives revelation for the area in which He has given responsibility and authority. *Look for revelation in areas of your responsibility.* Stay away from ego trips that motivate you to seek revelation for areas in which God has not yet placed you.

4. Walk together with others. Realize that until your guidance is confirmed, it should be regarded as what you *think* God is saying.

5. Realize that if you submit to God and resist the devil, he *must* flee from you! You can trust the guidance of the Holy Spirit to lead you into truth.

Add this tool of journaling to your "tool box" and you will mature in the grace of retaining revelation and the capacity of discerning God's voice. As you get ready to begin, you may wish to pray a prayer like this one:

"Father, grant me the grace to journal, in Jesus' great name. Teach me the skills of how to retain revelation and clearly discern the flow of Your voice. Lead me in Your wisdom applications of recording what You reveal. In Jesus' wonderful name, amen."

Now, let's just do it! Experience is always the best teacher!

Lesson Eleven

Nine Scriptural Tests

NOW LET'S NAIL THIS DOWN! Here is a list of nine scriptural tests by which we can test every revelation that we receive for accuracy, authority, and validity. The following truths are for all of us—whether you are an acknowledged Seer Prophet or everyday believer in the Lord Jesus Christ. Let's drop the plumb line of God's Word in our lives!

1. Does *the revelation edify, exhort, or console?* "But one who prophesies speaks to men for *edification* and *exhortation* and *consolation*" (1 Cor. 14:3). The end purpose of all true prophetic revelation is to build up, to admonish, and to encourage the people of God. Anything that is not directed to this end is not true prophecy. Jeremiah the prophet had to fulfill a negative commission, but even his difficult message contained a powerful and positive promise of God for those who were obedient (see Jer. 1:5,10). First Corinthians 14:26 sums it up best: "...Let all things be done for edification."

2. *Is it in agreement with God's Word?* "All scripture is given by inspiration of God..." (2 Tim. 3:16 KJV). True revelation

always agrees with the letter and the spirit of Scripture (see 2 Cor. 1:17-20). Where the Holy Spirit says "yea and amen" in Scripture, He also says yea and amen in revelation. He never, ever contradicts Himself.

3. *Does it exalt Jesus Christ?* "He will glorify Me, for He will take of Mine and will disclose it to you" (John 16:14). All true revelation ultimately centers on Jesus Christ and exalts and glorifies Him (see Rev. 19:10).

4. *Does it have good fruit?* "Beware of the false prophets, who come to you in sheep's clothing, but inwardly are ravenous wolves. You will know them by their fruits..." (Matt. 7:15-16). True revelatory activity produces fruit in character and conduct that agrees with the fruit of the Holy Spirit (see Eph. 5:9; Gal. 5:22-23). Some of the aspects of character or conduct that clearly are not the fruit of the Holy Spirit include pride, arrogance, boastfulness, exaggeration, dishonesty, covetousness, financial irresponsibility, licentiousness, immorality, addictive appetites, broken marriage vows, and broken homes. Normally, any revelation that is responsible for these kinds of results is from a source other than the Holy Spirit.

5. *If it predicts a future event, does it come to pass?* (See Deuteronomy 18:20-22.) Any revelation that contains a prediction concerning the future should come to pass. If it does not, then, with a few exceptions, the revelation is not from God. Exceptions may include the following issues:

   a. Will of person involved.

   b. National repentance—Ninevah repented, so the word did not occur.

   c. Messianic predictions. (They took hundreds of years to fulfill.)

d. There is a different standard for New Testament prophets than for Old Testament prophets whose predictions played into God's Messianic plan of deliverance.

6. *Does the prophetic prediction turn people toward God or away from Him?* (See Deuteronomy 13:1-5.) The fact that a person makes a prediction concerning the future that is *fulfilled* does not necessarily prove that person is moving by Holy Spirit-inspired revelation. If such a person, by his own ministry, turns others away from obedience to the one true God, then that person's ministry is false—even if he makes correct predictions concerning the future.

7. *Does it produce liberty or bondage?* "For you have not received a spirit of slavery leading to fear again, but you have received a spirit of adoption as sons by which we cry out, 'Abba! Father!'" (Rom. 8:15) True revelation given by the Holy Spirit produces liberty, not bondage (see 1 Cor. 14:33; 2 Tim. 1:7). The Holy Spirit never causes God's children to act like slaves, nor does He ever motivate us by fear or legalistic compulsion.

8. *Does it produce life or death?* "Who also made us adequate as servants of a new covenant, not of the letter but of the Spirit; for the letter kills, but the Spirit gives life" (2 Cor. 3:6). True revelation from the Holy Spirit always produces life, not death.

9. *Does the Holy Spirit bear witness that it is true?* "And as for you, the anointing which you received from Him abides in you, and you have no need for anyone to teach you; but as His anointing teaches you about all things, and is true and is not a lie, and just as it has taught you, you abide in Him" (1 John 2:27). The Holy Spirit within the believer always confirms true revelation from the Holy Spirit. The Holy Spirit is "the Spirit of Truth" (see John 16:13). He *bears*

witness to that which is true, but He rejects that which is false. This ninth test is the *most subjective* test of all the tests we've presented here. For that reason, it must be used in conjunction with the previous eight objective standards.

Add these nine scriptural tests together, and you will have just dropped an anchor to keep your boat steady and safe in times of turbulence and storms. The Word of God is the anchor for our soul!

Lesson Twelve

Testing the Spirits

DISCERNMENT IS DESPERATELY NEEDED IN the Body of Christ. We need a clear, clean stream of prophetic grace to flow in our day. The apostle John warns believers of every age:

> *Beloved, do not believe every spirit, but test the spirits to see whether they are from God, because many false prophets have gone out into the world. By this you know the Spirit of God: every spirit that confesses that Jesus Christ has come in the flesh is from God; and every spirit that does not confess Jesus is not from God; this is the spirit of the antichrist, of which you have heard that it is coming, and now it is already in the world* (1 John 4:1-3).

As we noted earlier, we have to test the spirits because prophecy, like the other gifts of the Spirit, is delivered through imperfect people. God has chosen to deliver the prophetic to the Church through the flawed and often immature vessels of humanity. Although "inscripturated revelation" was perfect and inerrant, "prophetic revelation" in the Church of Jesus Christ does not function on this level of inspiration. This is because prophecy is not our only source or way to hear God's voice. We have the living God dwelling in our hearts and the Holy

Spirit leading and guiding each of us each day. Perhaps most importantly, since Calvary, the seer and the prophet serve as a supportive and secondary role to the Bible, which is God's "more sure Word of prophecy" (see 2 Pet. 1:19), and to the indwelling Spirit of Christ in the heart of each believer.

Another reason discernment is needed is because God has chosen to speak through many people prophetically instead of using just one or two "perfected" people in a generation. Thus there is always the possibility of mixture in the revelatory word, because He chooses to use wounded people with clay feet (see 1 Cor. 14:29). At the same time, every believer has the basic tools to discern truth from falsehood for him or herself. The fact that revelation is open for judgment in this age proves its present, imperfect state. But remember the imperfect state of prophecy is directly linked to the imperfect state of the people who deliver it—not to an imperfect God!

Evil and deceived false prophets are not the major source of erroneous revelation to God's people today. Though this is on the rise; the vast majority of "diluted stuff" comes from sincere people who are simply adding their own insights to what started out as authentic, God-given revelation. They "add" to the nugget of God's prophetic message by drawing from things in their own human psyche, heart, emotions, concern, or sympathy. We need to learn to discern when God has stopped talking and man has continued on. Some of us over the years have called this "hamburger helper!" Whenever we share a revelation or vision that God has given us for someone else, we must be very careful to give what God has given and then clearly label or preface anything else we say as our own interpretations and views concerning that revelation or vision.

God's Word tells us that we must prove all things and hold fast to that which is good (see 1 Thess. 5:21). At all times we must seek the Lord's wisdom while refusing to use "wisdom" as an excuse for fear. We must be careful not to become offended at the genuine things that the Holy Spirit is doing, no matter how strange they may appear to us. Divine revelation and visionary experiences come in many different forms, and it is vital that we understand how to discern the true from the false.

Now I know that some of you are waiting for me to dish out "some of the deeper things" to you by this point. But from my perspective, I would be amiss not to make sure these foundational truths are laid well before taking us further on our "mystical journey."

With this in mind, we would do well to glance at some "wisdom issues" in the next short lesson. They will help us learn how to wisely discern the various forms of revelation we will encounter in our adventure with Christ.

Lesson Thirteen

Wisely Discerning Revelatory Encounters

WHAT WOULD YOU THINK IF you had a spiritual experience that made your hair stand on end? Would you write it off as absolutely satanic or "off the wall" because it didn't fit your theological code? Many people would and do. Supernatural encounters are real. The seer dimension into the spirit world is not something relegated to yesterday—it exists today and is on the rise! The question we must answer is: Do all such revelatory encounters come from the one true God or can there be other sources? How can we tell the source or nature of the spirit beings we encounter? What are the marks of a truly God-initiated encounter or revelatory experience?

There is only one dependable, unshakable guide through the minefield of supernatural encounters. In a world filled with spiritual voices of the new age and every other type and description, Christians need to know how to make their way through a spiritual field littered with hidden (and deadly) weapons of the enemy designed to wound or destroy the unwary and the undiscerning.

Entire segments of the Body of Christ have "written off" the supernatural aspects of God's Kingdom and His workings in the Church today because of fears about being deceived and led astray. Others have written it off due to excess, abuse, and the bad testimony left behind by lone rangers who are not accountable to anyone in the Body of Christ. The prophetic has been given a bad rap at times, but some of the wound has been self-inflicted. Nonetheless, God *does speak* to His people today and He is very capable of preserving us from harm and deception.

> [Jesus said] *For everyone who asks, receives; and he who seeks, finds; and to him who knocks, it will be opened. Now suppose one of you fathers is asked by his son for a fish; he will not give him a snake instead of a fish, will he? Or if he is asked for an egg, he will not give him a scorpion, will he? If you then, being evil, know how to give good gifts to your children, how much more will your heavenly Father give the Holy Spirit to those who ask Him?* (Luke 11:10-13)

What about it—can we trust our Father? Believe it or not, God wants us to hear His voice even more than we want to hear it! He is a gracious Father who gives good gifts to His children. What is the foundation that we must lay?

Stick close to Jesus. Seek Him. Love Him! Give our all to Him. James 4:8 says it this way: "Draw near to God and He will draw near to you." We could never overemphasize this point: Cultivate intimacy with God through a relationship with His only Son, Jesus Christ.

God is a Father and He can be trusted. If we ask Him for the things of the Holy Spirit in the name of Christ, He will give us the real thing, not a counterfeit. Nonetheless, there are many issues that we must consider when approaching this valuable subject of wisely judging revelatory encounters.

Some people create their own fear culture. Enough of that already! If you are a believer in the Lord Jesus Christ, you are connected to a loving Father who does not trick His kids or give them fake stuff. He can be trusted, and trust Him we will. Ask the Father and He will give you more of the Holy Spirit!

Lesson Fourteen

Safety in the Family

Let's backtrack for a moment and re-look at some basics in closing. God still speaks today through many different avenues including visions, dreams, and angelic visitations. Another one of these ways of the Holy Spirit is called "inner knowings." We simply know that we know that we know! He also speaks to us through His inner voice, external audible voice, by journaling, through His creation and other awesome ways and means. Yet our most important source of revelation is the *Logos* canon of Scripture. The only way we can accurately and safely interpret supernatural revelation of *any kind* is to ask God for the spirit of wisdom and understanding and to seek the counsel of the Lord.

Since the Bible is our absolute standard against which we must test *all* spiritual experiences, it should be obvious that we need to know and study God's Word. It is our only absolute, infallible, unchanging standard of truth. Just as we must learn to crawl before we learn to walk in the natural, so we must learn the ways of the *Logos*, the written Word of God, before we can learn to safely work with *Rhema*, the revealed "now" word of God. A solid and balanced working knowledge of the New Testament is the very minimum requirement as we begin to investigate *Rhema* revelation in-depth. Otherwise, we have no plumb line of measurement.

God has also ordained that we find safety in our relationship to a Bible-believing fellowship. Paul wrote to the Ephesians, "Submit yourselves one to another..." and described many of the areas of covering that God has placed in our lives (see Eph. 5:21 KJV). The Bible says, "...In the multitude of counselors there is safety" (Prov. 11:14 KJV). In an age of lawlessness, we find safety under the umbrella-like covering of the Lord, of His Word, and of the local church. We are not called to be proud religious rebels "doing our own thing." God has called us to be humble servants committed to a local expression of Christ's Body, diligently studying the Scriptures, praying daily, and being led by the Spirit of Truth into His purposes and individual will for our lives.

Though I am involved in many councils on national and international levels and have a somewhat recognized prophetic and intercessory voice, my family and I are regular members of a local spirit-filled fellowship. So what I put before you is not theory to me. It is walking in a form of simplicity and purity to Christ. We never outgrow the ABCs! With this in mind, we should all ask ourselves five basic questions in our quest to discern God's voice in the spirit realm:

1.   Am I regularly studying the Scriptures?

2.   Am I maintaining a life of prayer?

3.   Am I seeking purity, cleansing, and holiness in my life?

4.   Am I a worshipful member of a local Christian congregation?

5.   Am I committed to a few peer relationships that can speak into my life?

These building blocks must be firmly in place before we begin to investigate the principles of testing spiritual experiences. With these

ABCs in place, our next step is to "...examine everything carefully; hold fast to that which is good" (1 Thess. 5:21).

Let's now put into application the principles we have learned and let's ask the Lord for an increase in revelation, interpretation, and application! Remember, He wants you to hear His voice and know His prophetic ways—even more than you want to learn them. You can rely on the Holy Spirit! He is a great teacher.

With this in mind, let's get to it! Remember, journaling is simply another tool of The Lost Art of the Prophetic. But not anymore! It's time! Let's just do it!

With a Love for the Ways of God!

JAMES W. GOLL

My Personal Visionary Journal

*Your journal is a track record of your spiritual adventure,
not simply a diary to record daily activities.*

Date: _____

Time: _____

Location: _____

Type of Experience: _____

Dream, Vision, or Encounter:

_____

_____

_____

_____

_____

_____

_____

_____

_____

_____

_____

_____

_____

Is there a primary Scripture to relate to this experience?

_____

_____

Are you observing, participating, or the focus?

_____

_____

What is the primary feeling contained in the experience?

_____

_____

_____

_____

Possible Interpretation:

_____

_____

_____

_____

_____

_____

_____

Application and Reflection:

_____

_____

_____

_____

_____

_____

_____

Write a prayer related to your revelation:

_____

_____

_____

_____

_____

_____

_____

_____

*Why does God send dreams to unbelievers? Because He
wants to turn their hearts toward Him! God is unwilling
that anyone should perish.*

Date: _____

Time: _____

Location: _____

Type of Experience: _____

Dream, Vision, or Encounter:

_____

_____

_____

_____

_____

_____

_____

_____

_____

_____

_____

_____

Is there a primary Scripture to relate to this experience?

_____

_____

Are you observing, participating, or the focus?

_____

_____

What is the primary feeling contained in the experience?

_____

_____

_____

_____

Possible Interpretation:

_____

_____

_____

_____

_____

_____

_____

Application and Reflection:

_____

_____

_____

_____

_____

_____

_____

_____

Write a prayer related to your revelation:

_____

_____

_____

_____

_____

_____

_____

_____

_____

Pray for the Lord to release in our own day godly people of wisdom who can interpret the handwriting on the wall for our generation!

Date: _____

Time: _____

Location: _____

Type of Experience: _____

Dream, Vision, or Encounter:

_____

_____

_____

_____

_____

_____

_____

_____

_____

_____

_____

_____

_____

Is there a primary Scripture to relate to this experience?

_____

_____

Are you observing, participating, or the focus?

_____

_____

What is the primary feeling contained in the experience?

_____

_____

_____

_____

Possible Interpretation:

_____

_____

_____

_____

_____

_____

_____

Application and Reflection:

_____
_____
_____
_____
_____
_____
_____
_____

Write a prayer related to your revelation:

_____
_____
_____
_____
_____
_____
_____
_____

God likes playing hide and seek. We get to seek out the treasure
He has hidden for us! He loves this journey of hooking
us with revelation with the purpose of actually
reeling us into His very heart.

Date: _____

Time: _____

Location: _____

Type of Experience: _____

Dream, Vision, or Encounter:

_____

_____

_____

_____

_____

_____

_____

_____

_____

_____

_____

_____

Is there a primary Scripture to relate to this experience?

_____

_____

Are you observing, participating, or the focus?

_____

_____

What is the primary feeling contained in the experience?

_____

_____

_____

_____

Possible Interpretation:

_____

_____

_____

_____

_____

_____

_____

Application and Reflection:

_____

_____

_____

_____

_____

_____

_____

_____

Write a prayer related to your revelation:

_____

_____

_____

_____

_____

_____

_____

_____

Journaling is a tried and tested spiritual tool that will help you retain revelation and grow in your capacity to discern the voice of the Holy Spirit. I have tried it, and it works!

Date: _____

Time: _____

Location: _____

Type of Experience: _____

Dream, Vision, or Encounter:

_____

_____

_____

_____

_____

_____

_____

_____

_____

_____

_____

_____

Is there a primary Scripture to relate to this experience?

_____

_____

Are you observing, participating, or the focus?

_____

_____

What is the primary feeling contained in the experience?

_____

_____

_____

_____

Possible Interpretation:

_____

_____

_____

_____

_____

_____

_____

Application and Reflection:

_____

_____

_____

_____

_____

_____

_____

_____

Write a prayer related to your revelation:

_____

_____

_____

_____

_____

_____

_____

_____

*"You're not disciplined enough to have a spiritual discipline.
These are spiritual privileges."*

Date: _____

Time: _____

Location: _____

Type of Experience: _____

Dream, Vision, or Encounter:

_____

_____

_____

_____

_____

_____

_____

_____

_____

_____

_____

Is there a primary Scripture to relate to this experience?

_____

_____

Are you observing, participating, or the focus?

_____

_____

What is the primary feeling contained in the experience?

_____

_____

_____

_____

Possible Interpretation:

_____

_____

_____

_____

_____

_____

_____

Application and Reflection:

_____

_____

_____

_____

_____

_____

_____

Write a prayer related to your revelation:

_____

_____

_____

_____

_____

_____

_____

*The simple art of recording revelation may prove to be one of
the missing links in your own walk of hearing God's voice.
God speaks to His children much of the time!*

Date: _____

Time: _____

Location: _____

Type of Experience: _____

Dream, Vision, or Encounter:

_____

_____

_____

_____

_____

_____

_____

_____

_____

_____

_____

_____

Is there a primary Scripture to relate to this experience?

_____

_____

Are you observing, participating, or the focus?

_____

_____

What is the primary feeling contained in the experience?

_____

_____

_____

_____

Possible Interpretation:

_____

_____

_____

_____

_____

_____

_____

Application and Reflection:

_____

_____

_____

_____

_____

_____

_____

Write a prayer related to your revelation:

_____

_____

_____

_____

_____

_____

_____

_____

God cares about what transpires in our lives and has made
Himself available to each of us. He is
not out of touch or beyond reach.

Date: _____

Time: _____

Location: _____

Type of Experience: _____

Dream, Vision, or Encounter:

_____

_____

_____

_____

_____

_____

_____

_____

_____

_____

_____

_____

_____

Is there a primary Scripture to relate to this experience?

_____

_____

Are you observing, participating, or the focus?

_____

_____

What is the primary feeling contained in the experience?

_____

_____

_____

Possible Interpretation:

_____

_____

_____

_____

_____

_____

Application and Reflection:

_____

_____

_____

_____

_____

_____

_____

Write a prayer related to your revelation:

_____

_____

_____

_____

_____

_____

_____

What God did before, He wants to do again!
Right here, right now!

Date: _____

Time: _____

Location: _____

Type of Experience: _____

Dream, Vision, or Encounter:

_____

_____

_____

_____

_____

_____

_____

_____

_____

_____

_____

_____

Is there a primary Scripture to relate to this experience?

_____

_____

Are you observing, participating, or the focus?

_____

_____

What is the primary feeling contained in the experience?

_____

_____

_____

_____

Possible Interpretation:

_____

_____

_____

_____

_____

_____

_____

Application and Reflection:

_____

_____

_____

_____

_____

_____

_____

_____

Write a prayer related to your revelation:

_____

_____

_____

_____

_____

_____

_____

_____

*Praying, studying, fasting, worshiping—they are all
amazing spiritual privileges—with great benefits!*

Date: _____

Time: _____

Location: _____

Type of Experience: _____

Dream, Vision, or Encounter:

_____

_____

_____

_____

_____

_____

_____

_____

_____

_____

_____

_____

Is there a primary Scripture to relate to this experience?

_____

_____

Are you observing, participating, or the focus?

_____

_____

What is the primary feeling contained in the experience?

_____

_____

_____

_____

Possible Interpretation:

_____

_____

_____

_____

_____

_____

_____

_____

Application and Reflection:

_____

_____

_____

_____

_____

_____

_____

_____

Write a prayer related to your revelation:

_____

_____

_____

_____

_____

_____

_____

_____

The more you learn how to listen and recognize the voice of the Spirit of God, the more He will enable you to operate on multiple levels of insight.

Date: _____

Time: _____

Location: _____

Type of Experience: _____

Dream, Vision, or Encounter:

_____

_____

_____

_____

_____

_____

_____

_____

_____

_____

_____

_____

Is there a primary Scripture to relate to this experience?

_____

_____

Are you observing, participating, or the focus?

_____

_____

What is the primary feeling contained in the experience?

_____

_____

_____

_____

Possible Interpretation:

_____

_____

_____

_____

_____

_____

_____

Application and Reflection:

_____

_____

_____

_____

_____

_____

_____

_____

Write a prayer related to your revelation:

_____

_____

_____

_____

_____

_____

_____

_____

A great revival will come and the glory of the Lord will cover the earth as the waters cover the seas. Dreams and visions are a major part of the prophetic outpouring of God's great love in the Last Days!

Date: _____

Time: _____

Location: _____

Type of Experience: _____

Dream, Vision, or Encounter:

_____

_____

_____

_____

_____

_____

_____

_____

_____

_____

_____

Is there a primary Scripture to relate to this experience?

_____

_____

Are you observing, participating, or the focus?

_____

_____

What is the primary feeling contained in the experience?

_____

_____

_____

_____

Possible Interpretation:

_____

_____

_____

_____

_____

_____

_____

_____

Application and Reflection:

_____

_____

_____

_____

_____

_____

_____

_____

Write a prayer related to your revelation:

_____

_____

_____

_____

_____

_____

_____

_____

Some of our experiences are full of symbolism and others...
well, they are just flat out another dimension. God shows up
and shows off. When that happens, write with as much
emotive passion as possible!

Date: _____

Time: _____

Location: _____

Type of Experience: _____

Dream, Vision, or Encounter:

_____

_____

_____

_____

_____

_____

_____

_____

_____

_____

_____

Is there a primary Scripture to relate to this experience?

_____

_____

Are you observing, participating, or the focus?

_____

_____

What is the primary feeling contained in the experience?

_____

_____

_____

_____

Possible Interpretation:

_____

_____

_____

_____

_____

_____

_____

_____

Application and Reflection:

_____

_____

_____

_____

_____

_____

_____

_____

Write a prayer related to your revelation:

_____

_____

_____

_____

_____

_____

_____

*"Where are My Daniels? Where are My Esthers? Where are
My Josephs, and where are My Deborahs?"*

Date: _____

Time: _____

Location: _____

Type of Experience: _____

Dream, Vision, or Encounter:

_____

_____

_____

_____

_____

_____

_____

_____

_____

_____

_____

_____

Is there a primary Scripture to relate to this experience?

_____

_____

Are you observing, participating, or the focus?

_____

_____

What is the primary feeling contained in the experience?

_____

_____

_____

_____

Possible Interpretation:

_____

_____

_____

_____

_____

_____

_____

Application and Reflection:

_____
_____
_____
_____
_____
_____
_____
_____

Write a prayer related to your revelation:

_____
_____
_____
_____
_____
_____
_____
_____

The Holy Spirit is on a quest to find believers He can work with—believers who will dream God's dreams at any cost.

Date: _____

Time: _____

Location: _____

Type of Experience: _____

Dream, Vision, or Encounter:

_____

_____

_____

_____

_____

_____

_____

_____

_____

_____

_____

_____

Is there a primary Scripture to relate to this experience?

_____

_____

Are you observing, participating, or the focus?

_____

_____

What is the primary feeling contained in the experience?

_____

_____

_____

_____

Possible Interpretation:

_____

_____

_____

_____

_____

_____

_____

Application and Reflection:

_____

_____

_____

_____

_____

_____

_____

Write a prayer related to your revelation:

_____

_____

_____

_____

_____

_____

_____

*If the revelation is preserved, then another group, city, or
even generation can learn the lessons and
move forward themselves.*

Date: _____

Time: _____

Location: _____

Type of Experience: _____

Dream, Vision, or Encounter:

_____

_____

_____

_____

_____

_____

_____

_____

_____

_____

_____

_____

Is there a primary Scripture to relate to this experience?

_____

_____

Are you observing, participating, or the focus?

_____

_____

What is the primary feeling contained in the experience?

_____

_____

_____

_____

Possible Interpretation:

_____

_____

_____

_____

_____

_____

_____

Application and Reflection:

_____

_____

_____

_____

_____

_____

_____

Write a prayer related to your revelation:

_____

_____

_____

_____

_____

_____

_____

What do we do with the promises the Lord gives us?
They are worth more than any amount of money.

Date: _____

Time: _____

Location: _____

Type of Experience: _____

Dream, Vision, or Encounter:

_____

_____

_____

_____

_____

_____

_____

_____

_____

_____

_____

Is there a primary Scripture to relate to this experience?

_____

_____

Are you observing, participating, or the focus?

_____

_____

What is the primary feeling contained in the experience?

_____

_____

_____

_____

Possible Interpretation:

_____

_____

_____

_____

_____

_____

_____

Application and Reflection:

_____
_____
_____
_____
_____
_____
_____
_____

Write a prayer related to your revelation:

_____
_____
_____
_____
_____
_____
_____
_____

God wants to give us the keys of revelation so that we can unlock the meanings behind our dreams. It is the glory of a king to search out a matter! Be a king, and go search it out! This is your inheritance!

Date: _____

Time: _____

Location: _____

Type of Experience: _____

Dream, Vision, or Encounter:

_____

_____

_____

_____

_____

_____

_____

_____

_____

_____

_____

Is there a primary Scripture to relate to this experience?

_____

_____

Are you observing, participating, or the focus?

_____

_____

What is the primary feeling contained in the experience?

_____

_____

_____

_____

Possible Interpretation:

_____

_____

_____

_____

_____

_____

_____

Application and Reflection:

_____

_____

_____

_____

_____

_____

_____

Write a prayer related to your revelation:

_____

_____

_____

_____

_____

_____

_____

Sometimes, God asks a question or elicits a response—
not because He does not know the answer; rather,
God's questions are ultimately invitations to
greater intimacy with Him!

Date: _____

Time: _____

Location: _____

Type of Experience: _____

Dream, Vision, or Encounter:

_____

_____

_____

_____

_____

_____

_____

_____

_____

_____

_____

Is there a primary Scripture to relate to this experience?

_____

_____

Are you observing, participating, or the focus?

_____

_____

What is the primary feeling contained in the experience?

_____

_____

_____

_____

Possible Interpretation:

_____

_____

_____

_____

_____

_____

_____

Application and Reflection:

_____

_____

_____

_____

_____

_____

_____

_____

Write a prayer related to your revelation:

_____

_____

_____

_____

_____

_____

_____

_____

Before you go to sleep, toss up a simple prayer. Just declare,
"Here I am, Lord; I am ready to receive." He will come;
He will invade your space. Just receive!

Date: _____

Time: _____

Location: _____

Type of Experience: _____

Dream, Vision, or Encounter:

_____

_____

_____

_____

_____

_____

_____

_____

_____

_____

_____

_____

_____

Is there a primary Scripture to relate to this experience?

_____

_____

Are you observing, participating, or the focus?

_____

_____

What is the primary feeling contained in the experience?

_____

_____

_____

_____

Possible Interpretation:

_____

_____

_____

_____

_____

_____

_____

Application and Reflection:

_____

_____

_____

_____

_____

_____

_____

Write a prayer related to your revelation:

_____

_____

_____

_____

_____

_____

_____

Dreams do not explain the future—
the future will explain the dreams.

Date: _____

Time: _____

Location: _____

Type of Experience: _____

Dream, Vision, or Encounter:

_____

_____

_____

_____

_____

_____

_____

_____

_____

_____

_____

_____

_____

_____

Is there a primary Scripture to relate to this experience?

_____

_____

Are you observing, participating, or the focus?

_____

_____

What is the primary feeling contained in the experience?

_____

_____

_____

_____

Possible Interpretation:

_____

_____

_____

_____

_____

_____

_____

_____

Application and Reflection:

_____

_____

_____

_____

_____

_____

_____

_____

Write a prayer related to your revelation:

_____

_____

_____

_____

_____

_____

_____

_____

*I don't want to live an ordinary life and I am sure you
don't either. I want to live a life in the supernatural to such
an incredible degree that will cause people to say, "Behold!
There is a dreamer." Let's pursue the Master Dream Weaver
and His revelatory ways together!*

Date: _____

Time: _____

Location: _____

Type of Experience: _____

Dream, Vision, or Encounter:

_____
_____
_____
_____
_____
_____
_____
_____
_____
_____
_____

Is there a primary Scripture to relate to this experience?

_____

_____

Are you observing, participating, or the focus?

_____

_____

What is the primary feeling contained in the experience?

_____

_____

_____

_____

Possible Interpretation:

_____

_____

_____

_____

_____

_____

_____

_____

Application and Reflection:

_____
_____
_____
_____
_____
_____
_____

Write a prayer related to your revelation:

_____
_____
_____
_____
_____
_____
_____

Quietness can actually be a form of faith because it is the opposite of anxiety and worry.

Date: _____

Time: _____

Location: _____

Type of Experience: _____

Dream, Vision, or Encounter:

_____

_____

_____

_____

_____

_____

_____

_____

_____

_____

_____

_____

Is there a primary Scripture to relate to this experience?

_____

_____

Are you observing, participating, or the focus?

_____

_____

What is the primary feeling contained in the experience?

_____

_____

_____

_____

Possible Interpretation:

_____

_____

_____

_____

_____

_____

_____

Application and Reflection:

_____

_____

_____

_____

_____

_____

_____

Write a prayer related to your revelation:

_____

_____

_____

_____

_____

_____

_____

*What language do you speak? Whatever your language
is, the Holy Spirit will speak to you in that language.
We each have a personal walk and, in a sense, a
personal talk. Our spiritual alphabet, though similar,
is unique to each individual.*

Date: _____

Time: _____

Location: _____

Type of Experience: _____

Dream, Vision, or Encounter:

_____

_____

_____

_____

_____

_____

_____

_____

_____

_____

Is there a primary Scripture to relate to this experience?

_____

_____

Are you observing, participating, or the focus?

_____

_____

What is the primary feeling contained in the experience?

_____

_____

_____

_____

Possible Interpretation:

_____

_____

_____

_____

_____

_____

_____

Application and Reflection:

_____

_____

_____

_____

_____

_____

_____

_____

Write a prayer related to your revelation:

_____

_____

_____

_____

_____

_____

_____

_____

*Enter the Holy of Holies in your heart where Jesus the
Messiah lives. Yes, He has taken up residence within you!
He is there, and He is waiting to commune with you.*

Date: _____

Time: _____

Location: _____

Type of Experience: _____

Dream, Vision, or Encounter:

_____

_____

_____

_____

_____

_____

_____

_____

_____

_____

_____

Is there a primary Scripture to relate to this experience?

_____

_____

Are you observing, participating, or the focus?

_____

_____

What is the primary feeling contained in the experience?

_____

_____

_____

_____

Possible Interpretation:

_____

_____

_____

_____

_____

_____

_____

Application and Reflection:

_____
_____
_____
_____
_____
_____
_____
_____

Write a prayer related to your revelation:

_____
_____
_____
_____
_____
_____
_____
_____

The only way we can accurately and safely interpret supernatural revelation of any kind is to ask God for the spirit of wisdom and understanding and to seek the counsel of the Lord.

Date: _____

Time: _____

Location: _____

Type of Experience: _____

Dream, Vision, or Encounter:

_____

_____

_____

_____

_____

_____

_____

_____

_____

_____

_____

Is there a primary Scripture to relate to this experience?

_____

_____

Are you observing, participating, or the focus?

_____

_____

What is the primary feeling contained in the experience?

_____

_____

_____

_____

Possible Interpretation:

_____

_____

_____

_____

_____

_____

_____

Application and Reflection:

_____

_____

_____

_____

_____

_____

_____

_____

Write a prayer related to your revelation:

_____

_____

_____

_____

_____

_____

_____

_____

*When your dreams seem to fade away, press in— because
the God of dreams has not faded away. He is always there
waiting to embrace you and to expand your heart's capacity
to receive more of His Word, His will, and His ways.
When God seems silent, press in!*

Date: _____

Time: _____

Location: _____

Type of Experience: _____

Dream, Vision, or Encounter:

_____

_____

_____

_____

_____

_____

_____

_____

_____

_____

Is there a primary Scripture to relate to this experience?

_____

_____

Are you observing, participating, or the focus?

_____

_____

What is the primary feeling contained in the experience?

_____

_____

_____

_____

Possible Interpretation:

_____

_____

_____

_____

_____

_____

_____

_____

Application and Reflection:

_____

_____

_____

_____

_____

_____

_____

_____

Write a prayer related to your revelation:

_____

_____

_____

_____

_____

_____

_____

*The Lord, the Master Dream Weaver, has a word of
encouragement for you and for all of us: "I will be
your Helper!"*

Date: _____

Time: _____

Location: _____

Type of Experience: _____

Dream, Vision, or Encounter:

_____

_____

_____

_____

_____

_____

_____

_____

_____

_____

_____

_____

Is there a primary Scripture to relate to this experience?

_____

_____

Are you observing, participating, or the focus?

_____

_____

What is the primary feeling contained in the experience?

_____

_____

_____

_____

Possible Interpretation:

_____

_____

_____

_____

_____

_____

_____

_____

Application and Reflection:

_____

_____

_____

_____

_____

_____

_____

_____

Write a prayer related to your revelation:

_____

_____

_____

_____

_____

_____

_____

_____

Imagine being in the place where you are so sure that interpretations belong to God and so absolutely confident in His anointing that you could say to someone, "Tell your dream to me," and know that God would give you the interpretation!

Date: _____

Time: _____

Location: _____

Type of Experience: _____

Dream, Vision, or Encounter:

_____

_____

_____

_____

_____

_____

_____

_____

_____

_____

Is there a primary Scripture to relate to this experience?

_____

_____

Are you observing, participating, or the focus?

_____

_____

What is the primary feeling contained in the experience?

_____

_____

_____

_____

Possible Interpretation:

_____

_____

_____

_____

_____

_____

_____

Application and Reflection:

_____
_____
_____
_____
_____
_____
_____
_____

Write a prayer related to your revelation:

_____
_____
_____
_____
_____
_____
_____

Wage war with the dreams of insight that the Lord gives to you. Fight the enemy's plans in Jesus' name!

Date: _____

Time: _____

Location: _____

Type of Experience: _____

Dream, Vision, or Encounter:

_____

_____

_____

_____

_____

_____

_____

_____

_____

_____

_____

_____

_____

Is there a primary Scripture to relate to this experience?

_____

_____

Are you observing, participating, or the focus?

_____

_____

What is the primary feeling contained in the experience?

_____

_____

_____

_____

Possible Interpretation:

_____

_____

_____

_____

_____

_____

_____

Application and Reflection:

_____

_____

_____

_____

_____

_____

_____

Write a prayer related to your revelation:

_____

_____

_____

_____

_____

_____

_____

Often the Lord appears in various forms, motioning to us,
saying, "Catch Me if you can!"

Date: _____

Time: _____

Location: _____

Type of Experience: _____

Dream, Vision, or Encounter:

_____

_____

_____

_____

_____

_____

_____

_____

_____

_____

_____

_____

Is there a primary Scripture to relate to this experience?

_____

_____

Are you observing, participating, or the focus?

_____

_____

What is the primary feeling contained in the experience?

_____

_____

_____

_____

Possible Interpretation:

_____

_____

_____

_____

_____

_____

_____

_____

Application and Reflection:

_____
_____
_____
_____
_____
_____
_____
_____

Write a prayer related to your revelation:

_____
_____
_____
_____
_____
_____
_____
_____

Focusing the eyes of our heart upon God causes us to become inwardly still. It raises our level of faith and expectancy and results in our being more fully open to receive from God.

Date: _____

Time: _____

Location: _____

Type of Experience: _____

Dream, Vision, or Encounter:

_____

_____

_____

_____

_____

_____

_____

_____

_____

_____

_____

Is there a primary Scripture to relate to this experience?

_____

_____

Are you observing, participating, or the focus?

_____

_____

What is the primary feeling contained in the experience?

_____

_____

_____

_____

Possible Interpretation:

_____

_____

_____

_____

_____

_____

_____

Application and Reflection:

_____
_____
_____
_____
_____
_____
_____
_____

Write a prayer related to your revelation:

_____
_____
_____
_____
_____
_____
_____
_____

*If you seek God's face, God will give you the spirit
of understanding.*

Date: _____

Time: _____

Location: _____

Type of Experience: _____

Dream, Vision, or Encounter:

_____

_____

_____

_____

_____

_____

_____

_____

_____

_____

_____

_____

_____

_____

Is there a primary Scripture to relate to this experience?

_____

_____

Are you observing, participating, or the focus?

_____

_____

What is the primary feeling contained in the experience?

_____

_____

_____

_____

Possible Interpretation:

_____

_____

_____

_____

_____

_____

_____

Application and Reflection:

_____

_____

_____

_____

_____

_____

_____

Write a prayer related to your revelation:

_____

_____

_____

_____

_____

_____

_____

Write down a summary and keep it simple! The Holy Spirit will have a way of bringing back to your remembrance the details you might need later.

Date: _____

Time: _____

Location: _____

Type of Experience: _____

Dream, Vision, or Encounter:

_____

_____

_____

_____

_____

_____

_____

_____

_____

_____

_____

_____

_____

Is there a primary Scripture to relate to this experience?

_____

_____

Are you observing, participating, or the focus?

_____

_____

What is the primary feeling contained in the experience?

_____

_____

_____

_____

Possible Interpretation:

_____

_____

_____

_____

_____

_____

_____

Application and Reflection:

_____

_____

_____

_____

_____

_____

_____

_____

Write a prayer related to your revelation:

_____

_____

_____

_____

_____

_____

_____

_____

You were born to be a dreamer!

Date: _____

Time: _____

Location: _____

Type of Experience: _____

Dream, Vision, or Encounter:

_____

_____

_____

_____

_____

_____

_____

_____

_____

_____

_____

_____

_____

Is there a primary Scripture to relate to this experience?

_____

_____

Are you observing, participating, or the focus?

_____

_____

What is the primary feeling contained in the experience?

_____

_____

_____

_____

Possible Interpretation:

_____

_____

_____

_____

_____

_____

_____

Application and Reflection:

_____
_____
_____
_____
_____
_____
_____

Write a prayer related to your revelation:

_____
_____
_____
_____
_____
_____
_____

*If you are a believer in the Lord Jesus Christ, you are
connected to a loving Father who does not trick His kids
or give them fake stuff. He can be trusted, and trust
Him we will. Ask the Father and He will give you
more of the Holy Spirit!*

Date: _____

Time: _____

Location: _____

Type of Experience: _____

Dream, Vision, or Encounter:

_____

_____

_____

_____

_____

_____

_____

_____

_____

_____

Is there a primary Scripture to relate to this experience?

_____

_____

Are you observing, participating, or the focus?

_____

_____

What is the primary feeling contained in the experience?

_____

_____

_____

_____

Possible Interpretation:

_____

_____

_____

_____

_____

_____

_____

Application and Reflection:

_____

_____

_____

_____

_____

_____

_____

_____

Write a prayer related to your revelation:

_____

_____

_____

_____

_____

_____

_____

_____

Always put on your "mittens" of wisdom before trying to carry your cargo of revelation to its place of usefulness and purpose. Otherwise, it might spill on you!

Date: _____

Time: _____

Location: _____

Type of Experience: _____

Dream, Vision, or Encounter:

_____

_____

_____

_____

_____

_____

_____

_____

_____

_____

_____

_____

Is there a primary Scripture to relate to this experience?

_____

_____

Are you observing, participating, or the focus?

_____

_____

What is the primary feeling contained in the experience?

_____

_____

_____

_____

Possible Interpretation:

_____

_____

_____

_____

_____

_____

_____

Application and Reflection:

_____

_____

_____

_____

_____

_____

_____

Write a prayer related to your revelation:

_____

_____

_____

_____

_____

_____

_____

*In becoming still, you are not trying to do anything. You
simply want to be in touch with your Divine Lover, Jesus.*

Date: _____

Time: _____

Location: _____

Type of Experience: _____

Dream, Vision, or Encounter:

_____

_____

_____

_____

_____

_____

_____

_____

_____

_____

_____

_____

Is there a primary Scripture to relate to this experience?

_____

_____

Are you observing, participating, or the focus?

_____

_____

What is the primary feeling contained in the experience?

_____

_____

_____

_____

Possible Interpretation:

_____

_____

_____

_____

_____

_____

_____

Application and Reflection:

_____
_____
_____
_____
_____
_____
_____
_____

Write a prayer related to your revelation:

_____
_____
_____
_____
_____
_____
_____
_____

The seer dimension into the spirit world is not something relegated to yesterday—it exists today and is on the rise!

Date: _____

Time: _____

Location: _____

Type of Experience: _____

Dream, Vision, or Encounter:

_____
_____
_____
_____
_____
_____
_____
_____
_____
_____
_____
_____
_____
_____

Is there a primary Scripture to relate to this experience?

_____

_____

Are you observing, participating, or the focus?

_____

_____

What is the primary feeling contained in the experience?

_____

_____

_____

_____

Possible Interpretation:

_____

_____

_____

_____

_____

_____

_____

Application and Reflection:

_____

_____

_____

_____

_____

_____

_____

Write a prayer related to your revelation:

_____

_____

_____

_____

_____

_____

_____

Dreams are where space and time are pushed away,
where God allows our inner selves to see beyond and
behind the conscious plane and where possibilities and hopes,
as well as all our hidden monsters, come out,
come out wherever they are.

Date: _____

Time: _____

Location: _____

Type of Experience: _____

Dream, Vision, or Encounter:

_____

_____

_____

_____

_____

_____

_____

_____

_____

_____

_____

Is there a primary Scripture to relate to this experience?

_____

_____

Are you observing, participating, or the focus?

_____

_____

What is the primary feeling contained in the experience?

_____

_____

_____

_____

Possible Interpretation:

_____

_____

_____

_____

_____

_____

_____

Application and Reflection:

_____

_____

_____

_____

_____

_____

_____

_____

Write a prayer related to your revelation:

_____

_____

_____

_____

_____

_____

_____

_____

With too much detail you could miss the interpretation.
That is like not seeing the forest for the trees. Keep it simple.
Otherwise, you risk obscuring the meaning. Take the dream
to its simplest form and build on that.

Date: _____

Time: _____

Location: _____

Type of Experience: _____

Dream, Vision, or Encounter:

_____

_____

_____

_____

_____

_____

_____

_____

_____

_____

_____

Is there a primary Scripture to relate to this experience?

_____

_____

Are you observing, participating, or the focus?

_____

_____

What is the primary feeling contained in the experience?

_____

_____

_____

_____

Possible Interpretation:

_____

_____

_____

_____

_____

_____

_____

_____

Application and Reflection:

_____
_____
_____
_____
_____
_____
_____
_____

Write a prayer related to your revelation:

_____
_____
_____
_____
_____
_____
_____
_____

*What is God's purpose in using dream language? He wants
to not only spur us on to search for His message but also put
us in intimate touch with the Messenger—Himself. That is
His purpose—and His invitation.*

Date: _____

Time: _____

Location: _____

Type of Experience: _____

Dream, Vision, or Encounter:

_____

_____

_____

_____

_____

_____

_____

_____

_____

_____

_____

Is there a primary Scripture to relate to this experience?

_____

_____

Are you observing, participating, or the focus?

_____

_____

What is the primary feeling contained in the experience?

_____

_____

_____

_____

Possible Interpretation:

_____

_____

_____

_____

_____

_____

_____

Application and Reflection:

_____

_____

_____

_____

_____

_____

_____

_____

Write a prayer related to your revelation:

_____

_____

_____

_____

_____

_____

_____

_____

You can trust the guidance of the Holy Spirit to lead you into truth. If you submit to God and resist the devil, he must flee from you!

Date: _____

Time: _____

Location: _____

Type of Experience: _____

Dream, Vision, or Encounter:

_____

_____

_____

_____

_____

_____

_____

_____

_____

_____

_____

_____

Is there a primary Scripture to relate to this experience?

_____

_____

Are you observing, participating, or the focus?

_____

_____

What is the primary feeling contained in the experience?

_____

_____

_____

_____

Possible Interpretation:

_____

_____

_____

_____

_____

_____

_____

Application and Reflection:

_____

_____

_____

_____

_____

_____

_____

_____

Write a prayer related to your revelation:

_____

_____

_____

_____

_____

_____

_____

_____

You have not because you ask not! Ask for the interpretation!

Date: _____

Time: _____

Location: _____

Type of Experience: _____

Dream, Vision, or Encounter:

_____

_____

_____

_____

_____

_____

_____

_____

_____

_____

_____

_____

_____

Is there a primary Scripture to relate to this experience?

_____

_____

Are you observing, participating, or the focus?

_____

_____

What is the primary feeling contained in the experience?

_____

_____

_____

_____

Possible Interpretation:

_____

_____

_____

_____

_____

_____

_____

_____

Application and Reflection:

_____

_____

_____

_____

_____

_____

_____

_____

Write a prayer related to your revelation:

_____

_____

_____

_____

_____

_____

_____

_____

God has an awesome plan for your life and He wants to use dream language to speak to you. He wants to place the spirit of revelation upon your life and use you to bless and build up other believers. God wants to reveal Himself, His purposes, and His ways.

Date: _____

Time: _____

Location: _____

Type of Experience: _____

Dream, Vision, or Encounter:

_____

_____

_____

_____

_____

_____

_____

_____

_____

_____

_____

Is there a primary Scripture to relate to this experience?

_____

_____

Are you observing, participating, or the focus?

_____

_____

What is the primary feeling contained in the experience?

_____

_____

_____

_____

Possible Interpretation:

_____

_____

_____

_____

_____

_____

_____

Application and Reflection:

_____
_____
_____
_____
_____
_____
_____
_____

Write a prayer related to your revelation:

_____
_____
_____
_____
_____
_____
_____
_____

Take the time to gain understanding of the principles and metaphors of Scripture. Like the psalmist, meditate on them day and night. They can have many layers of meaning.

Date: _____

Time: _____

Location: _____

Type of Experience: _____

Dream, Vision, or Encounter:

_____

_____

_____

_____

_____

_____

_____

_____

_____

_____

_____

Is there a primary Scripture to relate to this experience?

_____

_____

Are you observing, participating, or the focus?

_____

_____

What is the primary feeling contained in the experience?

_____

_____

_____

Possible Interpretation:

_____

_____

_____

_____

_____

_____

_____

Application and Reflection:

_____

_____

_____

_____

_____

_____

_____

Write a prayer related to your revelation:

_____

_____

_____

_____

_____

_____

_____

*Dreams are indeed the supernatural communication of
Heaven—love letters filled with mysteries, intrigue,
and divine parables. Dream language is truly a
language of the ages.*

Date: _____

Time: _____

Location: _____

Type of Experience: _____

Dream, Vision, or Encounter:

_____

_____

_____

_____

_____

_____

_____

_____

_____

_____

_____

Is there a primary Scripture to relate to this experience?

_____

_____

Are you observing, participating, or the focus?

_____

_____

What is the primary feeling contained in the experience?

_____

_____

_____

_____

Possible Interpretation:

_____

_____

_____

_____

_____

_____

_____

Application and Reflection:

_____

_____

_____

_____

_____

_____

_____

Write a prayer related to your revelation:

_____

_____

_____

_____

_____

_____

_____

More than one dream in the same night is often just a different
look or version of the same message. If you experience
repetitive dreams, look for a common thread of meaning.

Date: _____

Time: _____

Location: _____

Type of Experience: _____

Dream, Vision, or Encounter:

_____

_____

_____

_____

_____

_____

_____

_____

_____

_____

_____

Is there a primary Scripture to relate to this experience?

_____

_____

Are you observing, participating, or the focus?

_____

_____

What is the primary feeling contained in the experience?

_____

_____

_____

_____

Possible Interpretation:

_____

_____

_____

_____

_____

_____

_____

Application and Reflection:

_____

_____

_____

_____

_____

_____

_____

_____

Write a prayer related to your revelation:

_____

_____

_____

_____

_____

_____

_____

The more you learn how to listen and recognize the voice of the Spirit of God, the more He will enable you to operate on multiple levels of insight. God is the master multitasker and He can enable you to be a multitasker as well!

Date: _____

Time: _____

Location: _____

Type of Experience: _____

Dream, Vision, or Encounter:

_____

_____

_____

_____

_____

_____

_____

_____

_____

_____

Is there a primary Scripture to relate to this experience?

_____

_____

Are you observing, participating, or the focus?

_____

_____

What is the primary feeling contained in the experience?

_____

_____

_____

_____

Possible Interpretation:

_____

_____

_____

_____

_____

_____

_____

Application and Reflection:

_____

_____

_____

_____

_____

_____

_____

_____

Write a prayer related to your revelation:

_____

_____

_____

_____

_____

_____

_____

_____

Remove external distractions so you can talk to God and listen to Him talk to you. Nothing takes the place of time alone with God!

Date: _____

Time: _____

Location: _____

Type of Experience: _____

Dream, Vision, or Encounter:

_____

_____

_____

_____

_____

_____

_____

_____

_____

_____

_____

_____

Is there a primary Scripture to relate to this experience?

_____

_____

Are you observing, participating, or the focus?

_____

_____

What is the primary feeling contained in the experience?

_____

_____

_____

_____

Possible Interpretation:

_____

_____

_____

_____

_____

_____

_____

Application and Reflection:

_____

_____

_____

_____

_____

_____

_____

Write a prayer related to your revelation:

_____

_____

_____

_____

_____

_____

_____

When it comes to spiritual matters, we are all helpless without Him. That is why He sent His Son Jesus to die on the cross for our sins, and why He sent the Holy Spirit to abide in the heart of every believer. God loves to help the helpless!

Date: _____

Time: _____

Location: _____

Type of Experience: _____

Dream, Vision, or Encounter:

_____

_____

_____

_____

_____

_____

_____

_____

_____

_____

_____

Is there a primary Scripture to relate to this experience?

_____

_____

Are you observing, participating, or the focus?

_____

_____

What is the primary feeling contained in the experience?

_____

_____

_____

_____

Possible Interpretation:

_____

_____

_____

_____

_____

_____

_____

_____

Application and Reflection:

_____

_____

_____

_____

_____

_____

_____

_____

Write a prayer related to your revelation:

_____

_____

_____

_____

_____

_____

_____

_____

You can listen on more than one level. You can listen to the heart of a person, you can listen to the realm of the soul, and you can listen to the Holy Spirit. All things are possible!

Date: _____

Time: _____

Location: _____

Type of Experience: _____

Dream, Vision, or Encounter:

_____

_____

_____

_____

_____

_____

_____

_____

_____

_____

_____

_____

Is there a primary Scripture to relate to this experience?

_____

_____

Are you observing, participating, or the focus?

_____

_____

What is the primary feeling contained in the experience?

_____

_____

_____

_____

Possible Interpretation:

_____

_____

_____

_____

_____

_____

_____

_____

Application and Reflection:

_____

_____

_____

_____

_____

_____

_____

Write a prayer related to your revelation:

_____

_____

_____

_____

_____

_____

_____

*God will speak to you with colloquial expressions that are
familiar to you but might not be to someone else.
God will speak to each of you accordingly.*

Date: _____

Time: _____

Location: _____

Type of Experience: _____

Dream, Vision, or Encounter:

_____
_____
_____
_____
_____
_____
_____
_____
_____
_____

Is there a primary Scripture to relate to this experience?

_____

_____

Are you observing, participating, or the focus?

_____

_____

What is the primary feeling contained in the experience?

_____

_____

_____

_____

Possible Interpretation:

_____

_____

_____

_____

_____

_____

_____

_____

Application and Reflection:

_____

_____

_____

_____

_____

_____

_____

Write a prayer related to your revelation:

_____

_____

_____

_____

_____

_____

_____

Always begin with the Scriptures. Let the Bible be its own
best commentary. God will never contradict His Word.

Date: _____

Time: _____

Location: _____

Type of Experience: _____

Dream, Vision, or Encounter:

_____
_____
_____
_____
_____
_____
_____
_____
_____
_____
_____
_____
_____

Is there a primary Scripture to relate to this experience?

_____

_____

Are you observing, participating, or the focus?

_____

_____

What is the primary feeling contained in the experience?

_____

_____

_____

_____

Possible Interpretation:

_____

_____

_____

_____

_____

_____

_____

_____

Application and Reflection:

_____

_____

_____

_____

_____

_____

_____

Write a prayer related to your revelation:

_____

_____

_____

_____

_____

_____

_____

*"Father, we know that dreams and their interpretations
belong to You. With honor coupled with a deep hunger, we
ask You to give us Your wisdom applications,
in Jesus' great name, Amen."*

Date: _____

Time: _____

Location: _____

Type of Experience: _____

Dream, Vision, or Encounter:

_____

_____

_____

_____

_____

_____

_____

_____

_____

_____

_____

Is there a primary Scripture to relate to this experience?

_____

_____

Are you observing, participating, or the focus?

_____

_____

What is the primary feeling contained in the experience?

_____

_____

_____

_____

Possible Interpretation:

_____

_____

_____

_____

_____

_____

_____

Application and Reflection:

_____

_____

_____

_____

_____

_____

_____

Write a prayer related to your revelation:

_____

_____

_____

_____

_____

_____

_____

All revelation is to be tested. You will make mistakes.
Accept that as a part of the learning process and go on.

Date: _____

Time: _____

Location: _____

Type of Experience: _____

Dream, Vision, or Encounter:

_____

_____

_____

_____

_____

_____

_____

_____

_____

_____

_____

_____

Is there a primary Scripture to relate to this experience?

_____

_____

Are you observing, participating, or the focus?

_____

_____

What is the primary feeling contained in the experience?

_____

_____

_____

_____

Possible Interpretation:

_____

_____

_____

_____

_____

_____

_____

_____

Application and Reflection:

_____

_____

_____

_____

_____

_____

_____

Write a prayer related to your revelation:

_____

_____

_____

_____

_____

_____

_____

*God is the Master Dream Weaver. Through dreams God
communicates directly with us concerning our destiny as well
as the destinies of our families, our nation, and our world.*

Date: _____

Time: _____

Location: _____

Type of Experience: _____

Dream, Vision, or Encounter:

_____

_____

_____

_____

_____

_____

_____

_____

_____

_____

_____

_____

Is there a primary Scripture to relate to this experience?

_____

_____

Are you observing, participating, or the focus?

_____

_____

What is the primary feeling contained in the experience?

_____

_____

_____

_____

Possible Interpretation:

_____

_____

_____

_____

_____

_____

_____

Application and Reflection:

_____
_____
_____
_____
_____
_____
_____
_____

Write a prayer related to your revelation:

_____
_____
_____
_____
_____
_____
_____
_____

Center on this moment of time and experience Jesus in it.
Silence the inner noise of voices, thoughts, pressures, etc.,
that otherwise would force their way to the top.

Date: _____

Time: _____

Location: _____

Type of Experience: _____

Dream, Vision, or Encounter:

_____

_____

_____

_____

_____

_____

_____

_____

_____

_____

_____

Is there a primary Scripture to relate to this experience?

_____

_____

Are you observing, participating, or the focus?

_____

_____

What is the primary feeling contained in the experience?

_____

_____

_____

_____

Possible Interpretation:

_____

_____

_____

_____

_____

_____

_____

_____

Application and Reflection:

_____

_____

_____

_____

_____

_____

_____

_____

Write a prayer related to your revelation:

_____

_____

_____

_____

_____

_____

_____

_____

God wants to make you fluent once again in dream
language, the mystical language of Heaven.

Date: _____

Time: _____

Location: _____

Type of Experience: _____

Dream, Vision, or Encounter:

_____

_____

_____

_____

_____

_____

_____

_____

_____

_____

_____

_____

Is there a primary Scripture to relate to this experience?

_____

_____

Are you observing, participating, or the focus?

_____

_____

What is the primary feeling contained in the experience?

_____

_____

_____

_____

Possible Interpretation:

_____

_____

_____

_____

_____

_____

_____

Application and Reflection:

_____
_____
_____
_____
_____
_____
_____
_____

Write a prayer related to your revelation:

_____
_____
_____
_____
_____
_____
_____

The Lord speaks mysteries, secrets, whose meaning is hidden
except to those who have a heart and soul to search it out.

Date: _____

Time: _____

Location: _____

Type of Experience: _____

Dream, Vision, or Encounter:

_____

_____

_____

_____

_____

_____

_____

_____

_____

_____

_____

_____

Is there a primary Scripture to relate to this experience?

_____

_____

Are you observing, participating, or the focus?

_____

_____

What is the primary feeling contained in the experience?

_____

_____

_____

_____

Possible Interpretation:

_____

_____

_____

_____

_____

_____

_____

Application and Reflection:

_____

_____

_____

_____

_____

_____

_____

_____

Write a prayer related to your revelation:

_____

_____

_____

_____

_____

_____

_____

_____

Terminology

Dream Symbols and Their Interpretations

The following material is not intended to be an official dictionary of definitions, but rather a tool to be flexibly used in the hands of believers under the leadership of the Holy Spirit. Thanks go to numerous pioneers who have blazed a trail in understanding these ways of God. People such as Kevin Connor, Herman Riffel, John Paul Jackson, Ira Milligan, Jane Hamon, Chuck Pierce, and others have indeed been forerunners for us all. Over time, you will grow in your interpretive grace and you will add some of your own understandings to the following dream symbols and their interpretations.

ACID: Bitter, offense, carrying a grudge, hatred, sarcasm.

ALLIGATOR: Ancient, evil out of the past (through inherited or personal sin), danger, destruction, evil spirit.

ALTAR: A symbol for sacrifice and for incense.

ANCHOR: Representation of safety and hope.

ARM: Represents God's power and strength.

ARMOR: A symbol of warfare.

ASHES: Memories, repentance, ruin, destruction.

AUTOMOBILE: Life, person, ministry.

AUTUMN: End, completion, change, repentance.

AXE: Represents warfare and judgment.

BABY: New beginning, new idea, dependent, helpless, innocent, sin.

BALANCE(S): Represents judgment.

BARN: Symbol for blessings.

BAT: Witchcraft, unstable, flighty, fear.

BEARD: Represents old age and wisdom.

BEAVER: Industrious, busy, diligent, clever, ingenious.

BED: Rest, salvation, meditation, intimacy, peace, covenant (marriage, natural or evil), self-made.

BICYCLE: Works, works of the flesh, legalism, self-righteousness, working out life's difficulties, messenger.

BIRD: Symbol of spirits, good or evil, see the parable of Jesus on the birds.

BLACK: Symbol of famine and death.

BLOOD: Symbol for sacrifice and for life (life is in the blood).

BLUE: Symbol of Heaven.

BOW: Usually represents judgment.

BREAD: Represents life.

BRICK: Represents slavery and human effort.

BRIDLE: Symbol of restraint, control.

BROTHER-IN-LAW: Partiality or adversary, fellow minister, problem relationship, partner, oneself, natural brother-in-law.

BROWN: Dead (as in plant life), repentant, born again, without spirit.

BULL: Persecution, spiritual warfare, opposition, accusation, slander, threat, economic increase.

BUTTERFLY: Freedom, flighty, fragile, temporary glory.

CAMEL: Represents servanthood, bearing the burden of others.

CANDLE: Symbol of light (Holy Spirit or the spirit of man).

CANDLESTICK: Represents the Church.

CAT: Self-willed, untrainable, predator, unclean spirit, bewitching charm, stealthy, sneaky, deception, self-pity, something precious in the context of a personal pet.

CATERPILLAR: Represents judgment and destructive powers.

CENSER: Symbol of intercession and worship.

CHAIN: Symbol of binding, oppression, punishment.

CHICKEN: Fear, cowardliness; hen can be protection, gossip, motherhood; rooster can be boasting, bragging, proud; chick can be defenseless, innocent.

CIRCLE: Symbol of eternity.

CITY: Symbol of security, safety, permanency, (cities of refuge).

CLOUD and **FIERY PILLAR:** Represents Divine presence, covering and guidance.

COLT: Represents bearing burden of others or could be a portrayal of stubbornness.

CORN (Oil and Wine): Represents blessings of God.

CROW (raven): Confusion, outspoken, operating in envy or strife, hateful, direct path, unclean, God's minister of justice or provision.

CUP: Symbol of life, health, or could represent death and evil.

CYMBAL: Symbol of vibration, praise, worship.

DEER: Graceful, swift, sure-footed, agile, timid.

DESERT: Desolation, temptation, solitude.

DOG: Unbelievers, religious hypocrites.

DOOR: An opening, entrance.

DOVE: Holy Spirit.

DRAGON: Satan.

DREAMING: A message within a message, aspiration, vision.

DROWNING: Overcome, self-pity, depression, grief, sorrow, temptation, excessive debt.

DRUGS: Influence, spell, sorcery, witchcraft, control, legalism, medicine, healing.

EIGHT: New beginnings.

EIGHT-EIGHT-EIGHT: The first resurrection saints.

ELEPHANT: Invincible or thick-skinned, not easily offended, powerful, large.

ELEVATOR: Changing position, going into the spirit realm, elevated, demoted.

ELEVEN: Incompleteness, disorder.

EYE(S): Omniscience, knowledge, sight, insight, foresight.

FACE: Character, countenance.

FALLING: Unsupported, loss of support (financial, moral, public), trial, succumb, backsliding.

FATHER: Authority, God, author, originator, source, inheritance, tradition, custom, satan, natural father.

FATHER-IN-LAW: Law, authoritative relationship based on law, legalism, problem authoritative relationship, natural father-in-law.

FEATHERS: Covering, protection.

FEET: Heart, walk, way, thoughts (meditation), offense, stubborn (unmovable), rebellion (kicking), sin.

FIFTY: Symbol of liberty, freedom, Pentecost.

FIG: Relates to Israel as a nation.

FIG LEAVES: Self-atonement, self-made covering.

FINGER: Feeling, sensitivity, discernment, conviction, works, accusation (as in pointing a finger), instruction.

FIRE: Presence of God, Holiness of God, purifying, testing.

FIVE: God's grace to man, responsibility of man.

FISH: Souls of men.

FLIES: Evil spirits, filth of satan's kingdom. Beelzebub = "lord of flies."

FLOOD: Judgment on sin and violence (the flood from Noah's time).

FLOWER: Fading glory of man.

FOREST: Symbol of nations.

FORTRESS: Protection, a stronghold.

FORTY: Symbol of testing, trial, closing in victory or defeat (Israel in Wilderness and Jesus in the desert).

FORTY-TWO: Israel's oppression, the Lord's advent to the earth.

FORTY-FIVE: Preservation.

FOUNTAIN: Source of life, refreshing.

FOUR: Represents worldwide, universal (as in four corners of the earth).

FOURTEEN: Passover, time of testing.

FOX: Cunning, evil men.

FRIEND: Self, the character or circumstance of one's friend reveals something about oneself; sometimes one friend represents another (look for the same name, initials, hair color); sometimes represents actual friend.

FROG: Demons, unclean spirits.

GARDEN: Growth and fertility.

GATE: A way of entrance, power, authority.

GOLD: Kingship, kingdom glory, God or gods.

GRANDCHILD: Heir, oneself, inherited blessing or iniquity, one's spiritual legacy, actual grandchild.

GRANDPARENT: Past, spiritual inheritance (good or evil), actual grandparent.

GRAPES: Fruit of the vine, cup of the Lord.

GRASS: Frailty of the flesh.

GRASSHOPPER: Destruction.

GREEN: Prosperity, growth, life.

HAMMER: Word of God.

HAND: Symbol of strength, power, action, possession.

HARP: Praise, worship to God.

HEAD: Authority, thoughts, mind.

HEART: Emotions, motivations, desires.

HELMET: Protection for thoughts, mind.

HEN: One who gathers, protects.

HILLS: Elevation, high, loftiness.

HORN: Power, strength, defense.

HORSE: Power, strength, conquest.

HOUSE: Home, dwelling place, the Church.

INCENSE: Prayer, intercessions and worship.

JEWELS: People of God.

KEY: Authority, power to bind or loose, lock or unlock.

KISS: Agreement, covenant, enticement, betrayal, covenant breaker, deception, seduction, friend.

KNEE: Reverence, humility.

LADDER: Christ connecting Heaven and earth.

LAMB: Humility, the Church, Christ.

LEAD: Weight, wickedness, sin, burden, judgment, fool, foolishness.

LEAF: Life amidst prosperity.

LEGS: Man's walk, man's strength.

LEOPARD: Swiftness, usually associated with vengeance.

LILIES: Beauty, majesty.

LION: Royalty and Kingship bravery, confidence.

LIPS: Witness.

MECHANIC: Minister, Christ, prophet, pastor, counselor.

MICE: Devourer, curse, plague, timid.

MILK: Foundational truth, nourishment.

MIRROR: God's Word or one's heart, looking at oneself, looking back, memory, past, vanity.

MISCARRIAGE: Abort, failure, loss, repentance, unjust judgment.

MONEY: Power, provision, wealth, natural talents and skills, spiritual riches, power, authority, trust in human strength, covetousness.

MONKEY: Foolishness, clinging, mischief, dishonesty, addiction.

MOON: Symbol of light in darkness, sign of the Son of Man.

MOTH: Symbol of destruction.

MOTHER: Source, Church, love, kindness, spiritual or natural mother.

MOTHER-IN-LAW: Legalism, meddler, trouble, natural mother-in-law.

MOUNTAIN: Kingdoms, dignity, permanence.

MOUTH: Witness, good or evil.

NAIL: Security, establish.

NECK: Force, loveliness, or inflexibility, meekness, rebellion.

NEST: Home, place to dwell.

NET: Symbol of a catcher as in the parables, catching men.

NINE: Judgment, finality.

NINETEEN: Barren, ashamed, repentant, selflessness, without self-righteousness; faith.

NOSE: Breath, discernment.

NUDITY: Uncovered or flesh, self-justification, self-righteousness, impure, ashamed, stubborn, temptation, lust, sexual control, exhibitionism, truth, honest, nature.

OIL: Holy Spirit, anointing.

ONE: God as a unity and as a source, new beginnings.

ONE HUNDRED: Fullness, full measure, full recompense, full reward; God's election of grace, children of promise.

ONE HUNDRED NINETEEN: The resurrection day; Lord's day.

ONE HUNDRED TWENTY: End of all flesh, beginning of life in the Spirit; divine period of probation.

ONE HUNDRED FORTY-FOUR: God's ultimate in creation.

ONE HUNDRED: Revival, ingathering, final harvest of souls.

ORANGE: Danger, great jeopardy, harm; a common color combination is orange and black, which usually signifies great evil or danger; bright or fire orange can be power, force, energy.

ONE THOUSAND: Maturity, full stature, mature service, mature judgment; divine completeness and the glory of God.

OVEN: Testing, or judgment.

PALACE: Heaven, royalty.

PALM TREE: Victory, worship.

PASTURE: Places of spiritual nourishment.

PEARL: Spiritual truth.

PEN/PENCIL: Tongue, indelible words, covenant, agreement, contract, vow, publish, record, permanent, unforgettable, gossip.

PIG: Ignorance, hypocrisy, religious unbelievers, unclean people, selfish, gluttonous, vicious, vengeful.

PILLAR: Strength, steadfastness, assistance.

PINK: Flesh, sensual, immoral, moral (as in a heart of flesh); chaste, a female infant.

PIT: Prison, oppression.

PLUMB LINE: Standards of God, measuring of a life.

PLOW: Breaking new ground.

PREGNANCY: In process, sin or righteousness in process, desire, anticipation, expectancy.

PUMPKIN: Witchcraft, deception, snare, witch, trick.

PURPLE: Royalty, wealth, prosperity.

RABBIT: Increase, fast growth, multiplication; hare can be satan and his evil spirits.

RACCOON: Mischief, night raider, rascal, thief, bandit, deceitful.

RAIN: Blessing, God's Word and revival.

RAINBOW: Covenant.

RAM: Sacrifice.

RAVEN: Evil, satan.

RED: Suffering, sacrifice or sin.

RINGS: Eternity, completion.

RIVER: Revival, refreshing.

ROACH: Infestation, unclean spirits, hidden sin.

ROBE: Covering, royalty.

ROCK: Christ our rock, stability.

ROD: Rule, correction, guidance.

ROOF: Covering, oversight.

ROOT: Spiritual source, offspring.

ROPE: Binding, bondage.

ROSE: Christ and His Church.

RUBIES: Value, worth, significance.

SALT: Incorruptibility, preserve from corruption, covenant.

SAND: Similar to seed, generations.

SAPPHIRE: Beauty, value.

SCORPION: Evil spirits, evil men; pinch of pain.

SEA: Wicked nations.

SERPENT: Satan and evil spirits.

SEVEN: Completeness, perfection.

SEVENTEEN: Spiritual order, incomplete, immature, undeveloped, childish, victory.

SEVENTY: Number of increase, perfected ministry.

SHEEP: Chant, the people of God, innocent.

SHIELD: Sign of protection.

SHOE: Sign of walking, protection for your walk.

SHOULDER: Bearing the burden of another, authority, rulership.

SISTER: Spiritual sister, Church, self, natural sister.

SIX-SIX-SIX: Sign of the Mark of the Beast, Antichrist.

SIXTEEN: Free-spirited, without boundaries, without law, without sin, salvation; love.

SIXTY: Pride.

SIXTY-SIX: Idol worship.

SIX HUNDRED: Warfare.

SKINS: Covering.

SMOKE: Blinding power.

SNOW: Spotlessness, radiance.

SPARROW: Small value but precious.

SPRING: New beginning, revival, fresh start, renewal, regeneration, salvation, refreshing.

STARS: Israel, generations.

STEPS: Signs of spiritual progress.

STONE: Might, permanence.

STORMS: Misfortune, difficulty, trials.

SUMMER: Harvest, opportunity, trial, heat of affliction.

SUN: Glory, brightness, light, Christ.

SWORD: Scriptures, Christ.

TEETH: Consuming power.

TEN: Law and order.

TENT: A temporary covering, not a permanent home.

TIGER: Danger, powerful minister (both good and evil).

TIN: Dross, waste, worthless, cheap, purification.

THIRTEEN: Sign of rebellion, backsliding, apostasy.

THIRTY: Maturity for ministry.

THIRTY-TWO: Covenant.

THIRTY-THREE: Promise.

THIRTY-FOUR: Naming of a son.

THIRTY-FIVE: Hope.

THIRTY-SIX: Enemy.

THIRTY-SEVEN: The Word of God.

THIRTY-EIGHT: Slavery.

THIRTY-NINE: Disease.

THREE HUNDRED: Faithful remnant (Gideon's army).

TONGUE: Language, speech.

TRAIN: Continuous, unceasing work, connected, fast, Church.

TRAP: Snare, danger, trick.

TREES: Nations, individuals, the Church.

TUNNEL: Passage, transition, way of escape, troubling experience, trial, hope.

TWELVE: Divine government, apostolic government.

TWENTY-ONE: Exceeding sinfulness, of sin.

TWENTY-FOUR: Symbol of Priesthood courses and order.

TWENTY-TWO: Light.

TWENTY-THREE: Death.

TWENTY-FIVE: The forgiveness of sins.

TWENTY-SIX: The gospel of Christ.

TWENTY-SEVEN: Preaching of the Gospel.

TWENTY-EIGHT: Eternal life.

TWENTY-NINE: Departure.

TWO: Sign for witness, testimony, or unity.

TWO HUNDRED: Insufficiency.

VAN: Family (natural or Church), family ministry, fellowship.

VINE: Symbol for Israel, Christ and His Church.

VULTURE: Sign of uncleanness and devourer.

WALL: Fortification, division, refuge.

WATCH: Prophetic, intercession, being on guard.

WATERS: Nations of earth; agitation, under-currents, cross-currents.

WELL: Places of refreshment, source of water of life.

WHEEL: Transport, a circle, speed, spiritual activity.

WINTER: Barren, death, dormant, waiting, cold, unfriendly.

WHIRLWIND: Hurricane, sweeping power, unable to resist.

WIND: Breath of life, power of God.

WINDOW: Blessings of Heaven, openness.

WINE: Holy Spirit.

WINESKIN: Spiritual structure.

WINGS: Protection, spiritual transport.

WOLF: Satan and evil, false ministries, and teachers.

WOMAN: Church, virgin or harlot.

WOOD: Humanity.

WRESTLING: Striving, deliverance, resistance, persistence, trial, tribulation, spirit attempting to gain control.

YELLOW: Gift, marriage, family, honor, deceitful gift, timidity, fear, cowardliness.

YOKE: Servitude, slavery, or fellowship.

Directions

EAST: Beginning: Law (therefore blessed or cursed); birth; first (Gen. 11:2; Job 38:24).

FRONT: Future or Now: (As in FRONT YARD) In the presence of; prophecy; immediate; current (Gen. 6:11; Rev. 1:19).

NORTH: Spiritual: Judgment; heaven; spiritual warfare (as in "taking your inheritance") (Prov. 25:23; Jer. 1:13-14).

LEFT: Spiritual: Weakness (of man), and therefore God's strength or ability; rejected. (Left Turn = spiritual change) (Judg. 3:20-21; 2 Cor. 12:9-10).

SOUTH: Natural: Sin; world; temptation; trial; flesh; corruption; deception (Josh. 10:40; Job 37:9).

RIGHT: Natural: Authority; power; the strength of man (flesh) or the power of God revealed through man; accepted. (Right Turn = natural change) (Matt. 5:29a, 30a; 1 Pet. 3:22).

WEST: End: Grace; death; last; conformed (Exod. 10:19; Luke 12:54).

BACK: Past: As in BACKYARD or BACKDOOR. Previous event or experience (good or evil); that which is behind (in time—for example, past sins or the sins of forefathers); unaware; unsuspecting; hidden; memory (Gen. 22:13; Josh. 8:4).

People/Relatives/Trades

BABY: New: Beginning; work; idea; the Church; sin; innocent; dependent; helpless; natural baby (1 Cor. 3:1; Isa. 43:19).

CARPENTER: Builder: Preacher; evangelist; laborer (good or evil); Christ (2 Kings 22:6; Isa. 41:7).

DOCTOR: Healer: Christ; preacher; authority; medical doctor, when naturally interpreted (Mark 2:17; 2 Chron. 16:12).

DRUNK: Influenced: Under a spell (i.e., under the influence of the Holy Spirit or a demon's spirit); controlled; fool; stubborn; rebellious; witchcraft (Eph. 5:18; Prov. 14:16).

EMPLOYER: Servants: Pastor, Christ; satan; actual employer, when naturally interpreted (Col. 3:22; 2 Pet. 2:19).

GIANT: Strongman: Stronghold, challenge; obstacle; trouble (Num. 13:32-33).

INDIAN: First: Flesh (as in "the old man"); firstborn; chief; fierce; savvy; native (Col. 3:9; Gen. 49:3).

POLICE: Authority: Natural (civil) or spiritual authority (pastors, etc.), good or evil; protection; angels or demons; an enforcer of a curse of the Law (Rom. 13:1; Luke 12:11).

Vehicles and Parts

AIRPLANE: Person or work: the Church; ministry; oversight (Soaring = Moved by the Spirit). (Hab. 1:8; Judg. 13:25).

JET: Ministry or Minister: Powerful; fast. (Passenger jet = Church; Fighter = Individual person). (Gen. 41:43; 2 Kings 10:16).

AUTOMOBILE: Life: Person; ministry (New car = New ministry or New way of life). (Gen. 41:43; 2 Kings 10:16).

AUTO WRECK: Strife: Contention; conflict, calamity; mistake or sin in ministry (as in "failure to maintain right-of-way"). (Nah. 2:4).

BICYCLE: Works: Works of the flesh (not of faith); self-righteousness; messenger. (Gal. 5:4; Gal. 5:19).

BOAT: Church or personal ministry: (Sailboat = moved by the Spirit; Powerboat = powerful or fast progress) (Gen. 6:16; 1 Tim. 1:19).

BRAKES: Stop: Hindrance; resist; wait. (Acts 16:6-7; 2 Pet. 2:14).

HELICOPTOR: Ministry: Personal; individual; the Church; versatile; stationary (when unmoving). (2 Tim. 4:2; Rom. 8:14).

MOTORCYCLE: Individual: Personal ministry; independent; rebellion; selfish; pride; swift progress. 2 Pet. 2:10; 1 Sam. 15:23).

PICKUP TRUCK: Work: Personal ministry or natural work. (1 Chron. 13:7; Gal. 6:5).

REARVIEW MIRROR: Word: (Driving backward using the rearview mirror = operating by the letter of the Word instead of by God's Spirit); legalistic; looking back (2 Cor. 3:6; Gen. 19:26).

RAFT: Adrift: Without direction; aimless; powerless. (Eph. 4:14).

TRACTOR: Powerful work: Slow but powerful ministry. (Acts 1:8; Acts 4:33).

TRACTOR-TRAILOR: Large burden: Ministry; powerful and/or large work (truck size is often in proportion to the burden or size of the work).

Miscellaneous

ANKLES: Faith: Weak ankles = weak faith; unsupported; undependable. (Ezek 47:3).

ARM: Strength or weakness: Savior; deliverer; helper; aid; reaching out. (Isa. 52:10; Ps. 136:12).

BANK: Secure: Church; dependable; safe; saved; sure (as in "you can bank on it"); reserved in Heaven. (Luke 19:23; Matt. 6:20).

BINOCULARS: Insight: Understanding; prophetic vision; future event. (John 16:13; 2 Cor. 3:13,16).

BLEEDING: Wounded: Hurt, naturally or emotionally; dying spiritually; offended; gossip; unclean. (Ps. 147:3; Prov. 18:8).

BLOOD TRANSFUSION: Change: Regeneration; salvation; deliverance. (Titus 3:5; Rom. 12:2).

BRIDGE: Faith: Trial; way; joined. (Gen. 32:22; 1 Cor. 10:13).

BUTTER: Works: Doing (or not doing) the Word or will of God; deceptive motives; words; smooth. (Ps. 55:21; Prov. 30:33).

CALENDAR: Time: Date: event; appointment. (Hos. 6:11).

CARDS: Facts: Honesty (as in "putting all your cards on the table"); truth; expose or reveal; dishonest; cheat; deceitful. (Rom. 12:17).

CARNIVAL: Worldly: Exhibitionism; divination; competition. (Acts 16:16; Luke 21:34).

CHAIR: Position: Seat of authority; rest. (Esther 3:1; Rev. 13:2).

CHECK: Faith: The currency of the Kingdom of God; provision; trust. (Heb. 11:1; Mark 4:40).

CHOKING: Hinder: Stumbling over something (as in "that's too much to swallow"); hatred or anger (as in "I could choke him!") (Mark 4:19).

CHRISTMAS: Gift: Season of rejoicing; spiritual gifts; a surprise; good will. (Luke 11:13; 1 Cor. 14:1).

CLOSET: Private: Personal, prayer; secret sin; hidden. (Matt. 6:6; Luke 8:17).

COFFEE: Bitter or Stimulant: Repentance; reaping what one has sown; desire for revenge (bitter envying). (Num. 9:11; Job 13:26).

DITCH: Habit: Religious tradition; addition; lust; passion. (Matt 15:14; Ps. 7:15).

DOMINOES: Continuous: Chain reaction. (Lev. 26:37).

EARTHQUAKE: Upheaval: change (by crisis), repentance; trial; God's judgment; disaster; trauma. (Acts 16:26; Isa. 29:6).

ECHO: Repetition: Gossip, accusation; voice of many; mocking. (Luke 23:21).

EGG: Idea: New thought; plan; promise; potential. (Luke 11:12; 1 Tim. 4:15).

FENCE: Barrier: Boundaries; obstacles; religious traditions; doctrines; inhibitions. (Gen. 11:6; Jer. 15:20).

GARBAGE (DUMP): Rejected: Hell; evil; vile; corruption. (Mark 9:47-48; 1 Cor. 9:27).

GASOLINE: Fuel: Prayer, inflammatory; gossip; contention; danger. (Jude 20; Prov. 26:20-21).

GLOVES: Covering: Protection; save; careful (as in "handle with kid gloves"). (Ps. 24:3-4; 1 Tim. 4:4-5).

MOWED GRASS: Chastisement: Sickness; financial need or distress; emotional and mental depression or anguish. (Amos 7:1-2; 1 Cor. 11:30-32).

GRAVEYARD: Hidden: Past; curse; evil inheritance; hypocrisy; demon. (Matt. 23:27; Luke 11:44).

GRAVEL PIT: Source: The Word of God; abundant supply. (Deut. 8:9; 2 Tim. 2:15).

MUDDY ROAD: Flesh: Man's way; lust; passion; temptation; difficulty caused by the weakness of the flesh. (Ps. 69:2; Isa. 57:20).

IRONING: Correction: Change; sanctification; exhorting; teaching righteousness; God's discipline; pressure (from trials). (Eph. 5:27).

LADDER: Ascend or Descend: Escape; enable; way; steps. (Gen. 28:12-13; John 3:13).

LIPS: Words: Seduction; speech. (Prov. 7:21; Prov. 10:19).

MAP: Directions: Word of God; correction; advice. (Prov. 6:23).

MICROPHONE: Voice: Authority; ministry; influence. (Matt. 10:27).

MIRROR: Word or one's Heart: God's Word; looking back; memory, past; vanity; Moses' Law. (1 Cor. 13:12; Prov. 27:19).

NEWSPAPER: Announcement: Important event; public exposure; news; gossip. (Luke 8:17).

OVEN: Heart: Heat of passion; imagination; meditation; judgment. (Hos. 7:6; Ps. 21:9).

PAINTBRUSH: Covering: (house painter's brush: regeneration: remodel, renovate; love. Artist's paint brush: Illustrative; eloquent; humorous; articulate.) (1 Pet. 4:8; Titus 3:5).

PARACHUTING: Leave: Bail out; escape; flee; saved. (2 Cor. 6:17; Jer. 50:28).

PERFUME: Seduction: Enticement; temptation; persuasion; deception. (Prov. 7:7,10,13; Eccles. 10:1).

PIE: Whole: Business endeavors; part of the action. (Luke 12:13).

PLAY: Worship: Idolatry; covetousness; true worship; spiritual warfare; strife; competition. (Col. 3:5; 1 Cor. 9:24).

POSTAGE STAMP: Seal: Authority; authorization; small or seemingly insignificant, but powerful. (Esther 8:8; John 6:27).

POT/PAN/BOWL: Vessel: Doctrine; traditions; a determination or resolve; form of the truth; a person. (Rom. 2:20; Jer. 1:13).

RADIO: Unchangeable: Unbelief; unrelenting; contentious; unceasing; tradition. (Prov. 27:15).

RAILROAD TRACK: Tradition: Unchanging; habit; stubborn; gospel. (Mark 7:9,13; Col. 2:8).

RAPE: Violation: Abuse of authority; hate; desire for revenge; murder. (2 Sam. 13:12,14-15; Deut 22:25-26).

REFRIGERATOR: Heart: Motive; attitude; stored in heart; harbor. (Matt. 12:35; Mark 7:21-22).

ROCKING CHAIR: Old: Past, memories; meditation; retirement; rest. (Jer. 6:16).

ROLLER COASTER: Unstable: Emotional instability; unfaithfulness; wavering; manic-depressive; depression; trials; excitement. (Isa. 40:4; James 1:6-8).

ROLLER SKATES: Speed: Fast; swift advancement or progress. (Rom. 9:28).

ROUND (shape): Spiritual: (A round face, ring, building, etc) Grace; mercy; compassion; forgiveness. (Lev. 19:27).

SEA COAST: Boundary: Flesh (which contains and limits the spirit of man); limitations; weights. (Jer. 5:22; Jer. 47:6-7).

SHOVEL: Tongue: Prayer; confession; slander; dig; search; inquire. (2 Kings 3:16-17; Deut. 23:13).

SKIING: Faith: (Water or snow skiing) Supported by God's power through faith; fast progress. (John 6:19, 21; Matt. 14:29-31).

SLEEP: Unconscious: Unaware; hidden or covered; ignorance; danger; death. (Isa. 29:10; Rom. 13:11).

SMILE: Friendly: Kindness; benevolent; without offense; seduction. (Prov. 18:24).

SQUARE: Legalistic: (Square eyeglasses, buildings, etc.) Religious or religion; no mercy; hard or harsh; of the world. (Lev. 19:9).

SWEEPING: Cleaning: Repentance; change; removing obstacles. (2 Cor. 7:1; 2 Cor. 7:11).

SWIMMING: Spiritual: Serving God; worship; operating the gifts of the Spirit; prophecy. (Ezek. 47:5; Eph. 3:8).

FALSE TEETH: Replacement: Wisdom or knowledge gained through experience or previous failures; logical reasoning; tradition. (Rom. 5:3-4; Col. 2:8).

TOOTHACHE: Trial: Unfaithful; no faith; unbelief. (Tooth = Wisdom; Ache = Suffering; Broken = Potential pain, i.e. when pressure is applied.) (Prov. 25:19).

TELEVISION: Vision: Message; prophecy; preaching; news; evil influence; wickedness. (Num. 24:16; Dan. 2:19).

THUNDER: Change or Without Understanding: (Of what the Spirit is saying or of the signs of the times). Dispensational change (i.e., a change in the way God deals with His people); warning of impending judgment or trouble. (John 12:28-29; Ps. 18:13).

TITLE/DEED: Ownership: Authorization; possession. (Gen. 23:20).

TREE STUMP: Unbelief; roots; tenacious; obstacle; immovable; hope. (Job 14:7-9).

URINATING: Spirit: Full bladder = Pressure. Compelling urge; temptation (such as sexual lust or strife); Bladder Infection or Cancer = Offense: Enmity. (Prov. 17:14).

WASHCLOTH: Truth: Doctrine; understanding. (Dirty cloth = False doctrine: Insincere apology; error.) (Ps. 51:7; Job 14:4).

WATERMELON: Fruit: The fruit of good or evil works; the pleasures of sin. (Seeds = Words; Water = Spirit; Sweetness = Strength; Green = Life; Red = Passion; Yellow = Gifts) (Num. 11:5; Prov. 1:31).

WESTERN: Frontier: ("The wild west," a western movie, etc.) Pioneer, spiritual warfare; boldness; challenge. (Deut. 20:10; Josh. 3:4).

About James W. Goll

Dr. James W. Goll is the president of Encounters Network, director of Prayer Storm, and coordinates Encounters Alliance, a coalition of leaders. He is the Founder of the God Encounters Training E-School of the Heart and has shared Jesus in more than 40 nations worldwide. Teaching and imparting the power of intercession and prophetic ministry, exalting Christ Jesus, and living a life filled with the Holy Spirit is His passion.

For More Information

James and Michal Ann Goll were married for 32 years before her graduation into Heaven in 2008. They are the parents of four wonderful young adults who all love and serve Jesus. James continues to live in Franklin, Tennessee.

James has also produced numerous study guides on subjects such as Equipping in the Prophetic, Blueprints for Prayer, and Empowered for Ministry, all available through the Encounters Resource Center.

Additional Books by James W. and Michal Ann Goll

The Lost Art of Intercession

The Lost Art of Pure Worship

The Lost Art of Practicing His Presence

The Call for the Elijah Revolution

The Coming Prophetic Revolution

Women on the Frontlines: A Call to Courage

Compassion: The Call to Take Action

A Call to the Secret Place

A Radical Faith

Intercession

God's Power in You

The Reformer's Pledge

The Beginner's Guide to Hearing God

The Beginner's Guide to Signs, Wonders and the Supernatural Life

Exploring the Gift and Nature of Dreams

Discovering the Seer in You

Empowered Women

Empowered Prayer

Prayer Storm

God Encounters

Prayer Storm Study Guide

Praying for Israel's Destiny

A Radical Faith Study Guide

The Coming Israel Awakening

The Seer 40 Day Devotional Journal

Shifting Shadows of Spiritual Experiences

Deliverance from Darkness Study Guide

The Coming Prophetic Revolution

Adventures in the Prophetic

Deliverance from Darkness

The Prophetic Intercessor

Angelic Encounters

Dream Language

The Seer

For More Information Contact:

Encounters Network

P.O. Box 1653
Franklin, TN 37075

Office Phone: 615-599-5552

Office Fax: 615-599-5554

For orders call: 1-877-200-1604

For more information, to sign up for weekly email communiqués, or to view over 200 free video and audio messages, visit the following web sites:

www.encountersnetwork.com

www.prayerstorm.com

www.compassionacts.com

www.jamesgoll.com

www.GETSchool.com

www.ENMedia.com

E-Mail: info@encountersnetwork.com

info@prayerstorm.com

prayer@encountersnetwork.com

IN THE RIGHT HANDS, THIS BOOK WILL CHANGE LIVES!

Most of the people who need this message will not be looking for this book. To change their lives, you need to put a copy of this book in their hands.

> *But others (seeds) fell into good ground, and brought forth fruit, some a hundred-fold, some sixty-fold, some thirty-fold* (Matthew 13:8).

Our ministry is constantly seeking methods to find the good ground, the people who need this anointed message to change their lives. Will you help us reach these people?

> *Remember this—a farmer who plants only a few seeds will get a small crop. But the one who plants generously will get a generous crop* (2 Corinthians 9:6).

EXTEND THIS MINISTRY BY SOWING
3 BOOKS, 5 BOOKS, 10 BOOKS, OR MORE TODAY,
AND BECOME A LIFE CHANGER!

Thank you,

Don Nori Sr., Founder
Destiny Image
Since 1982